100 Ideas for Early Years Practitioners

Outstanding Practice

Lucy Peet

B L O O M S B U R Y

Published 2013 by Bloomsbury Education

Bloomsbury Publishing plc

50 Bedford Square, London, WC1B 3DP

www.bloomsbury.com

Bloomsbury is a registered trademark of Bloomsbury Publishing Plc

978-1-4729-0633-5

3 5 7 9 10 8 6 4 2

Typeset by Fakenham Prepress Solutions, Fakenham, Norfolk, NR21 8NN

Printed and bound by CPI Group (UK) Ltd, Croydon, CR0 4YY

To view more of our titles please visit www.bloomsbury.com

To Team Peet, especially Jamie, whom I love very much.
Thank you for all your love and help.

Other titles in the 100 Ideas for Early Years Practitioners series:

100 Ideas for Early Years Practitioners: School Readiness
by Claire Ford

Other Early Years titles available from Bloomsbury:

Creative Planning in the EYFS: Pirates and the Seaside
by Lucy Peet

Creative Planning in the EYFS: Castles and Dragons
by Lucy Peet

Creative Planning in the EYFS: Spring
by Lucy Peet

Creative Planning in the EYFS: Autumn
by Lucy Peet

Contents

Acknowledgements viii
Introduction ix
How to use this book x

Ideas
1 Know your place 2
2 Helping hands 3
3 Line up! Line up! 4
4 Bonjour, Monsieur! 6
5 But I'm hungry now! 7
6 I can put my coat on! 8
7 Tidy-up music 9
8 Cloakroom monitors 10
9 Topical groups 11
10 Singing the register 12
11 Quiet please! 13
12 Coloured words 14
13 Personal placemats 15
14 Shy shared reader 16
15 Show and tell 17
16 This is my culture 18
17 That's my spot! 20
18 Fidgeting about! 21
19 What's mine is my own! 22
20 Who's taken my red pen, AGAIN? 23
21 Pick a pencil case! 24
22 Graffiti table 25
23 Roll up, roll up! 26
24 Chalk maps 27
25 Tidy silhouettes 28
26 Encouraging independent writing 29
27 Easy display of writing 30
28 Colour mixing for the squeamish! 31
29 Easy painty writing 32
30 Invisible graffiti 34
31 Sign up, sign up! 35
32 It's my turn next! 36
33 What do I need to take home? 37
34 That's my job! 38

35	No room!	39
36	Pass it on!	40
37	Listen carefully	42
38	Shadow maps	43
39	Coordinating coordinates!	44
40	Amateur archaeologists	45
41	Iceberg ahoy!	46
42	Stained ice windows	47
43	Marshmallow igloos	48
44	Cereal castles	49
45	Sliding shapes	50
46	What am I?	51
47	Washing line pictures	52
48	Which one am I?	53
49	It's all in the detail!	54
50	Hear it, draw it	56
51	Eat the alphabet	57
52	Waiter, waiter!	58
53	Hard hat helpers	59
54	Traffic lights	60
55	Show me, show me!	61
56	Hold it up!	62
57	Hungry Zippy	63
58	Clever Cow	64
59	Clock watching	65
60	Trust me, tell me	66
61	I can read that!	67
62	Noise slider	68
63	Counting sounds	69
64	Response partners	70
65	Stars in their eyes	71
66	Jigsaw experts	72
67	Remember, remember	73
68	Medical needs	74
69	Going home timetable	75
70	Topical help	76
71	Odd one out	77
72	Dotty about the dot chart	78
73	Standing straight!	79
74	My button family	80
75	Character 'king of the castle'	82
76	Let's go fishing	83
77	Size doesn't matter – shape does!	84
78	Bingo!	86
79	Guess who!	87
80	Make a shape!	88
81	The first one to fetch...	89

82	Outdoor motoring maths	90
83	Listening, turning, pointing...'Over there!'	91
84	Stand on something...blue!	92
85	100 square outdoor bingo	93
86	Outdoor orienteering	94
87	Posting postcards	96
88	The moving bus	97
89	The free workforce!	98
90	Personal effects	99
91	Get ready for summer!	100
92	What's on the whiteboard today?	101
93	Observing in order	102
94	Planning for everyone	103
95	Involving parents/carers	104
96	Morning challenges	105
97	Journey sticks	106
98	Sticky colour strips	107
99	My tree	108
100	People lines	109

Acknowledgements

I would like to say a big thank you to all the people who I have worked with and learned from in schools over the last 15 years. I have seen such excellent practice and been a part of such great teams it has been a continual learning process in every setting, but none more so than at Lowe's Wong Infant School in Nottinghamshire. I am privileged to work with brilliant practitioners, particularly those dedicated to Foundation Stage (yes, that means you and your team, Erica!).

In particular I would like to thank Phil Judge, Vanessa Platt and Aly Speed for being inspirational headteachers, each with a passion for educating the youngest children and believing in the possibility of being outstanding in the early years.

Thank you also to Evie and Poppy, my own early years children at home. It is their energy, enthusiasm and love of life which inspires me to keep thinking of new ideas!

A good teacher is remembered forever, and not just for the actual lessons they taught. The musical ideas in this book are dedicated to Miss Pamela Cook, my music teacher and choral director of Cantamus Girls' Choir for over 40 years. Miss Cook gave us all the belief that with hard work and dedication any of the teenage girls under her care could achieve whatever we wanted. At her funeral in July, 2013 over 400 current and previous choir members aged between 13 and 50 joined a full service in Southwell Minster to sing in her honour. Thank you Miss Cook – it was a privilege to be one of your pupils.

Introduction

Teaching is a challenging profession requiring dedication, perseverance, understanding, boundless energy and a good sense of humour, but the rewards are great. All teachers will have had special moments or special children that have made them stop, smile and realise why they chose teaching as a career. Adults working every hour possible in an early years setting, who are frequently covered in paint, dribble, glue and sand (among other liquids) do not do their job for the huge salary! Working with children in the early years may be the greatest privilege of all; you are part of the incredibly steep learning curve that young children make in the first months of their school life. I believe good early years practitioners to be particularly highly skilled. It is an incredible challenge to become the significant adult in the life of a three- or four-year-old child who has made perhaps a handful of relationships in their entire life, especially when this four year old is one of a group of 30.

The best practitioners in the early years have similar characteristics. These include a view of the whole child, an understanding of child development, excellent organisational skills, good time management, a friendly approach and above all a feeling that what won't kill them will make them stronger! It is possible to develop these characteristics to improve early years practice, and through implementing some of the 100 ideas in this book, the skills and knowledge relating to these characteristics will become embedded.

The ideas in this book have all been tried, tested and work well in a variety of early years settings. There are ideas for how to organise a setting, plan routines and daily activities and how to use resources and staff. There are ideas linked to planning, to extend outdoor provision, for PSE, numeracy, literacy and topic, and other quirky ideas to keep you sane, such as how to safeguard your register pens!

Please dip in and out of this book as you see fit, and try to incorporate some of these ideas into your daily and weekly routines and experiences as a skilled early years practitioner. As you are reading this book, you are clearly interested in improving the outcomes for these littlest people in our schools, as am I! Let's move all our provision from good to outstanding, as the children deserve.

How to use this book

This book includes quick, easy, practical ideas for you to dip in and out of, in order to move your practice in the early years from 'good' to 'outstanding'.

Each idea includes:

- A catchy title, easy to refer to and share with your colleagues
- A quote from a practitioner or child describing their experiences of the idea that follows, or a problem they may have had that using the idea solves
- A summary of the idea in bold, making it easy to flick through the book and identify an idea you want to use at a glance
- A step-by-step guide to implementing the idea.

Each idea also includes one or more of the following:

Teaching tip

Practical tips and advice for how and how not to run the activity or put the idea into practice; problems you might come across and how to solve them.

Taking it further

Ideas and advice for how to extend the idea, develop it further, or set it as homework.

Bonus idea ★

There are up to 12 bonus ideas in this book that are extra exciting and extra original to make your teaching extra outstanding!

100 Ideas for Early Years Practitioners

Outstanding Practice

Know your place

"When we were asked to sit on the carpet the noisy children always sat together and made it difficult for me to concentrate. I was always worried about who would sit next to me."

When each child has a position of their own on the carpet to sit in every time, it not only reassures the worried child and divides the unruly, it also helps a practitioner to remember names, target questions and dismiss individual children to activities quickly.

At first, allow a cohort of children to choose their own places on the carpet in front of you. After a few sessions consider the places of the children, and give each child a place that is relevant to their learning style, for example:

- Children who need a lot of 'wriggle room' or those who are left handed should be seated at the edges of the group, or on the left hand side to allow room to write with their dominant hand.
- Taller, more mature children who listen well may be suited to the back row.
- Less secure or younger children may be suited to a position right under the practitioner's nose, so they can be frequently drawn in to the discussion with a gentle touch or quiet comment.
- Children who are easily distracted may be seated between two calm children who will remain focused and will not join in with any naughtiness.

Helping hands

"Every day someone is chosen to be the teacher's helper. It's a really exciting job; I can't wait for it to be my turn!"

One or two children are chosen to be the 'helping hands' for the day. This idea works well for even the youngest children to foster a sense of responsibility and teamwork.

As helping hands, their job may include taking the registers to the office, collecting books, carrying a message to another class or being at the front and back of each line. The names of the next pair of helping hands are chosen at random from a box by the previous helping hands and the children see it is a very fair selection process.

- Create a small, lidded box, decorated with sparkly foil, jewels or glitter to indicate its special status.
- Give each child a small card with their name on it. Invite each child to come to the front and put their name in the box. This is an important part of the routine – the children must know that their name is in the box.
- On the first morning, explain to the children that you are going to select two children from the box to be helping hands for the day. Model closing your eyes and selecting a card with a flourish!
- Put the selected name cards into a bulldog clip to separate them from the rest of the group, explaining that they will not have a turn again until all the cards are used up.
- Give a simple task to the new helping hands immediately to consolidate their role.
- The following morning, the helping hands from the previous day select a new card each from the box, and pass the role on.

Taking it further

Create badges, sashes or waistcoats for the helping hands to wear all day. This will get them noticed as they carry out their duties around the setting, encouraging other adults to ask them about their role and other children to aspire to be a helping hand too!

3

Line up! Line up!

"I can keep the children focused well on the carpet or during a lesson, but when I ask them to line up it seems that they become much noisier and their behaviour disintegrates straight away! This is a nightmare if we have to walk through the setting in a line, for instance, to an assembly."

Points of transition in the session can often be times of poor behaviour, particularly if the children are required to move about. This idea will help to make a routine task more interesting and it also helps to maintain order, a calm environment and to improve the children's listening skills. If the children begin by listening well, walking sensibly to line up and standing quietly in a line they are more likely to move about quietly too.

Teaching tip

When dismissing children from the carpet to different activities, ask them to remain seated whilst you tell all the children where they are going. If some children move to their activity before others it is difficult for the children remaining to hear what you are saying.

A frequent point of improvement from lesson observation is how to maintain order and to retain silence whilst instructing different children to move to different activities in the session. To keep the children listening quietly, change the method of asking them to line up or go to their activity. As always, ensure that all of the children are listening silently before you begin. If someone begins to chat, stop speaking, look at them, and wait for silence again before beginning. Use a quiet voice so that they have to *really* listen, and specifically request that a particular group line up, for example request that all of the girls line up. Try some of these different requests:

'Line up quietly if you are...'

- ...wearing black socks
- ...four years old
- ...sitting on the front row
- ...have a brother.

To extend this further, use two criteria, for example: 'Line up if you are...a girl who is five or a boy who is having sandwiches today.'

If someone in the line of children begins to talk, call them back to the carpet and involve them in the 'listening for' criteria again. Look carefully at the remaining children and choose criteria to reduce the number of boys, vary the age or height of the line, or separate two chatting children. This is an excellent method of behaviour management without repeatedly naming an unruly child.

Bonus idea ★

A PSE/art idea: Play lining up or grouping as a PSE activity by giving the children different criteria. For example, line up in height order; stand in groups of the same eye or hair colour. Ask the children not to speak during the game, or select 'leaders' to direct the other children to the correct places. This can also support a topic such as 'Ourselves', or before an art task such as observational drawing and self-portraits. It may be useful to let each child hold a small mirror.

Taking it further

When doing P.E., or something similar where children are moving between different activities in a kind of 'circuit', this idea ensures they move smoothly between each one. Stop all the children together, and tell each group to point to the activity they are going to move to next. When all the children are pointing at something, instruct them to, 'Follow your finger and your leader to the next activity and wait'. This ensures that all children walk sensibly at the same time, and know where they are headed.

Bonjour, Monsieur!

"Every day I wonder what language we are going to speak when we get to school. It's exciting to see which flag is on the board, especially when it's one from my country."

It can be difficult in some settings to introduce the children to other cultures and countries. By adopting the language of another country each day, simply to greet each other and take the register, the children become aware that other people may be different from themselves. It also reassures children with English as an additional language (EAL) that their home language is valued at school.

Begin by using the different languages that are spoken by children or the families of children in your setting. Ask the children for different ways of saying 'good morning' and 'good afternoon' and write these on large cards, or create a whiteboard page containing the greetings and displaying relevant images of flags or places in other countries.

Taking it further

Further extend the use of foreign languages in the setting by introducing simple counting, songs and rhymes or ways to make basic requests like 'sandwiches please'. Invite native speakers of different languages to visit the setting to speak to the children and learn simple nouns to support the topic. Labelling objects around the setting in different languages will also support children with EAL.

- Before you begin the register, model the greeting to the children, for example: 'Buenos Dias'.
- Explain that this is how people who speak Spanish say 'Good morning' – if you have a Spanish-speaking child in the class, ask them if they would like to demonstrate.
- Take the register, saying, 'Buenos Dias' to each child and encouraging them to say it back.
- Put a picture of the Spanish flag on the board, and explain that when the children see that flag the morning greeting will be 'Buenos Dias'.
- Extend this activity to other countries, greetings and flags.

But I'm hungry now!

"I love eating fruit at school but sometimes I'm hungry before the teacher says it's snack time. I wish I could just eat it whenever I like."

When establishing routines for small children it can be supportive to have snack or milk time as a group. This family-style environment encourages poorer eaters to try different foods and it is helpful to eat together.

Explain to the children that the snack is going to be put out at the start of the session and that they can help themselves whenever they feel hungry. Include the children when deciding what the 'rules' for this will be, for example:

- Everyone is still only to have one piece of snack each – just because there is a bowlful does not mean there are two or three for everyone.
- The snack must be eaten sitting down at the snack table.
- There are only four chairs (or however many you feel will work) at the snack table, so if it is full then they must come back later.
- There will be a basket of name cards/photographs at the snack table, one for each child. When they have eaten their snack they should post their card in the post box. This will help the adult in the setting to encourage all children to eat their snack during the session.
- Some children may be allergic to some snack foods and may not be able to eat some of the snacks provided. If this occurs with a particular snack simply return to a 'group snack time' with adult supervision on this occasion to prevent any allergic reactions to food.

Teaching tip

Watch carefully for any children avoiding snack time. If this happens, manage the timings a little, by saying, for example, 'Please can the yellow table go to the snack area first this morning'. If there is still a 'reluctant eater' try going to the snack area with the child and eating your snack with them.

7

I can put my coat on!

"My life as a practitioner is made much easier at playtime or outdoor session when the children can put their own coat or shoes on. I just wish that some of them would learn at home!"

If you are the sole adult responsible for a group of small children it can seem like it takes forever to get them all dressed to go outside. The display and subsequent public recognition for learning how to put on and fasten coats and shoes is a very successful method of encouraging the parents and carers to help at home.

Teaching tip

Send a brief note home at the beginning of a holiday explaining to the parents and carers that they are being given a 'homework challenge' to spend a little time each day practising putting on coats and shoes independently – practise makes perfect!

This idea works best when the cloakroom or pegs are in a relatively public place, or near a window.

- Attach some large sheets of paper to the wall of the cloakroom and draw a large outline of a shoe or a coat.
- Make sure you include the heading – 'I can put my shoes (or coat) on by myself!' in big lettering over the picture.
- Take a photograph of each child proudly wearing their shoes or coat in front of the outline or wherever is most suitable.
- When they are able to dress themselves independently, put their photograph on the display.
- Remind the children to tell their parent/carer to look at the photograph each time they drop off or pick up.
- Pester power will work positively in this case, as each child (and parent/carer) will want to get their photograph on the display as soon as possible!

Tidy-up music

"When it's really noisy in the unit and children are playing in lots of different areas it can be difficult to make them all hear me when it is time to tidy up. Since I started using the 'tidy-up music' the end of each session has been much more organised!"

By playing a clearly recognised piece of music at the end of each session the children will learn to stop playing and begin to tidy away as soon as they hear the music. This will save your voice and help tidy-up time run quickly and smoothly.

When you have decided on a piece of music, make sure you have it on CD so that it is easy to find, easy to play and easy to put it on 'repeat track'.

- Play the music to the children. Discuss how it makes them feel – it could be something chaotic like 'Flight of the Bumblebee' by Rimsky-Korsakov or something tranquil like 'The Swan' by Saint-Saens.
- Explain to the children that this music is going to be like a signal. As soon as they hear it they are to stop whatever they are doing, wherever they are, and to begin tidying away.
- At first you will need to repeat the music to give the children enough time to clear away their activities, but after a while you will be able to reduce the time as they learn to tidy away more efficiently.
- Praise children who spring into action each time the music is played – by reinforcing the behaviour you want, you will reduce occurrences of the type of behaviour you do not want.

Taking it further

Play the music in all areas of the setting so that all the children understand that it means tidy up time. If you have a robust CD player for outdoors you could use it to tidy up after outdoor activities too or to signal the end of the session in the playground without raising your voice.

Cloakroom monitors

"I don't like going into the cloakroom to hang my coat up – it's always a really big squash and the bigger ones always shove me so I can't see my peg. Then my coat always gets pushed off its hook anyway".

Some children are born organisers, and with support will 'police' many areas and routines in your settings for you. By choosing a couple of monitors for your cloakroom they will ensure that the pushing and shoving that sometimes occurs is minimised and that the cloakroom area stays tidy.

Select the monitors carefully – if you choose a particularly bossy child this can backfire as no one likes to be given orders! Try to choose children who are quietly sensible and who are popular with the other children.

- Talk with the entire group about hanging their coats up at the start of each session – ask them what the problems are.
- Encourage the children to describe how they would ideally like the cloakroom to be.
- You can suggest ideas: 'Each child will have a peg they can reach (take their heights into account) with a clear name label.' And the children can suggest others: 'No one will push anyone, we will be patient in the small space.'
- If this talking session is done skillfully, the children will be involved in solving the problem and will be far more likely to follow new rules.
- The next time the children arrive at the door of the cloakroom, ensure that the monitors are already in place.
- Allow three or four children at a time into the area to hang up their coat. The monitors will signal to the others when it is their turn to enter, and will also help anyone struggling to put on or take off their coat.

Topical groups

"I always name my groups as creatively as possible! My favourite was during a 'food' topic where I smiled each time I said, 'Fish, chips and peas, please line up for lunch!' Sometimes the children self-select group names that couldn't be more appropriate – I remember a really wriggly 'worms' group and a particularly naughty table of 'monkeys'!"

It is useful for organisational purposes to be able to identify the children in the setting through different groups. Among other things, it allows a practitioner to identify several children at once or request a small group to carry out a task, for example 'Red group please wash your hands!'.

Using group names related to the topic widens children's vocabulary and also helps the practitioner to plan activities accordingly. In a setting with parallel groups try to use the same names in both rooms/sessions. This makes identification on planning much easier. Decide how you would like to group the children, for example: by age, term of intake, where they sit at the tables, friendship groups, learning style or attainment.

- Discuss group names with the children and compile a list of possibilities.
- Consider the topic and choose related names. For example, a topic on 'wheels' may have groups such as cars, lorries, buses and bicycles.
- Explain to the children that each group will make a sign and little badges/hats/medals with their group on. (This works best if it is a group where the same children attend the same session).
- Allocate each group a name, or let the children vote for their favourite.

Teaching tip

When deciding on group names, be creative and have fun with the names. When choosing names for groups try to use criteria to help you to remember. For example, if you are naming maths groups who sit on tables grouped by attainment, use shape names in order of the number of sides – 'circles' need support, 'hexagons' need extending. The same can be done for number of vehicles' wheels, types of animals or order of colours in the rainbow.

Singing the register

"For some children, saying 'Good morning' in front of a large group can be quite intimidating. I find that when I sing the register all the children join in with more confidence".

Choose a simple tune to sing the register to each day. At first the children can echo the phrase sung by the practitioner. As they become more confident, try simple call-and-answer songs where they use your name in greeting.

To the tune of 'Frère Jacques' sing each child's name. Allow a moment after your request so that the child can answer back by repeating the phrase you used.

- Sing, 'He-llo, E-vie'.
- Encourage Evie to echo the phrase, 'He-llo, E-vie', exactly copying the words and tune you used.
- Sing the following child's name, 'He-llo, Sa-am' (echoed by Sam).
- Continue through the register, 'He-e-e-llo Po-ppy' ('Hello Poppy').
- 'Hello Jack' ('Hello Jack').
- After these four phrases you will have reached the end of 'Frère Jacques', so begin again.

Quiet please!

"As a newly-qualified practitioner I found one of the most challenging things was to get the attention of the children when they were all busy. I ended up repeatedly saying, 'Quiet please! Please listen!' When I started the singing technique it was very effective – all the children joined in!"

It can be difficult to be heard above a noisy group of children, or to gain the attention of a group who are busily engaged in different tasks. By singing a simple and repetitive tune the children will come to recognise it as a signal to stop what they are doing and pay attention to the adult.

Do not be put off by this idea if you think you cannot sing! The children are not going to give marks out of ten – it is simply the change of tone and timbre to your normal speaking voice which will cause them to take notice.

- Stand in a place where you are visible to all children.
- Make eye contact with any children or groups of children who you think may not pay attention the first time.
- Sing a simple song or repeated phrase to inform the children it is time to stop and listen.
- If the song has an echo, for example 'Frère Jacques', and the children are required to repeat the phrase back, then they are more likely to turn to face you and join in.
- For example, sung to 'Frère Jacques':
  'Are you ready? (Are you ready)
  Listening? (Listening)
  Sitting on the carpet, (Sitting on the carpet)
  Listening, (Listening)'
- Change the words in line three to suit the occasion – standing behind chairs/standing in a line/sitting at your table.

Teaching tip

Other methods of gaining the attention of a large group can be more appropriate to different circumstances and ages of children. Standing with a hand raised invites other children to raise their hands and to be silent. This works well in assemblies or when the children are lined up on the playground. Using a repeated clap pattern, a bell or tambourine will let children know that you wish to speak, but remember to accompany this with a stance and facial expression clearly indicating to them you are waiting for silence!

Coloured words

"When I have to look at the board to copy I sometimes lose my place and can't remember which line I am on. If I ask the teacher which word to write down she says the one beginning with 'p', but then there is more than one and I don't know which one to choose!"

When writing on a board, flip chart or whiteboard for children to look at or copy, use alternate colour pens for each line so that the children know which line they are on next and can find their place easily.

Taking it further

When encouraging children to write independently it is useful to create a simple word bank of five or ten words. Write these words in a list on the board where all children can see them, and number each word. When the children are looking for a word and are not sure which it is, it is simple for the adult to say, 'Bethlehem is number seven' and for the children to find and copy the word from there.

If you are writing some keywords for the children to use in their writing, use different colour pens where possible. If there are words beginning with the same initial sound ensure that these at least are in different colours. This makes it easy to say to a child: 'It's the word beginning with "p", in green'. This is a very useful technique for doing handwriting for children to copy.

It is also possible to differentiate by task by asking the children to write only the words or sentences of a particular colour.

In addition to using different colours you may wish to add a little picture to show what the word is. This works well with nouns for writing.

Bonus idea

Many children find print on a white background very stark and it can be difficult to read. Research has shown that the clearest contrast is blue text on a pale yellow background. Consider photocopying onto cream or yellow paper instead of white, or changing the background page colour on the interactive whiteboard to yellow and the text to blue.

Personal placemats

"I find that I am often writing the same phoneme or numeral for children to copy several times during the same session. When I made them each a placemat with the letters on that we were using that week they didn't come to ask for help as often."

By creating a laminated placemat for each child to keep in the place where they work they can refer to it when necessary to find the phonemes and numbers they need independently.

It is possible to download many different word boards similar to those described below from the internet to print out. Do not be taken in by the idea that these look more attractive – they may not have the specific words the children need for their topic! Have the confidence to make and use your own.

- On an A4 sheet of paper write or type out the phonemes and numerals required by your children. Link these to the phonics taught if relevant.
- In small groups, allow the children to decorate or colour in the letters and symbols on the sheet to personalise it.
- Add their full name in letters large enough to copy over with a dry wipe pen.
- Laminate each placemat.
- Give them back to the children and play the 'point to' game – identify different phonemes and ask the children to point to them as quickly as possible!
- Keep these personal placemats in a suitable place for the children to access each time they want to write their name, letters, sounds or numerals.

Taking it further

Create simple placemats related to different topics and subjects for use in the setting. For example, on the number table have a set of placemats showing shapes and their names, or colours and numerals. When you are introducing a new topic, for example animals, make a set of placemats containing animal pictures and clearly written name labels for the children to use in their play, for example in the vet surgery or pet shop.

Shy shared reader

"I like reading a book that I've seen before – it's like I get a head start and can tell the other children what might happen."

For shy or reluctant children, reading or sharing a book in a group can be intimidating. If these children have seen the book before they are more confident and are able to contribute to a discussion, with support. It may be that the book you have chosen for the group to read is a direct response to the interests of the most reluctant reader.

Teaching tip

If you have a child who is reluctant to participate in story time, invite them to choose the book to be shared. If you know that they have a special interest in a particular subject try to gather books on the subject or containing the characters they like. Put these together in a special box and make time each session for the child to choose a book and bring it to you to be read together. Use this book as the story time book and encourage the child to talk about why they like it.

- Identify one or more books you will be sharing either at story time or as part of a guided/shared reading session.
- Decide which children would benefit from a prior look at the book; maybe those who are quiet in a group, or those who struggle to share a book and identify the characters or storyline.
- Give the children a copy of the book to take home and share with an adult the week before you are going to look at it with the other children. Alternatively, organise a small reading group to look at the chosen book before reading it with the larger group.
- Model talking about the book; identifying characters, talking about the setting and predicting the plot.
- The following week when sharing the book with the group, target questions and invite observations from the identified children who were given the support earlier. This will scaffold their contributions and increase their confidence.

Show and tell

"For show and tell, it often ends up that the same child brings in an endless supply of toys. How can I encourage the quieter children to have a turn without disappointing the more confident?"

Having a rota or timetable, for which children are invited to show and tell each day or week, ensures that all children have an equal opportunity to show an object from home or talk about something that is important to them.

For some parents and carers show and tell can be a cause of anxiety – when is it their child's turn, what do they bring, what do they say? Ensure that you have explained the process of show and tell, if necessary through a brief note home at the beginning of term.

- Explain to the children that they are invited to bring in an object or photograph from home to talk about and show to the other children in the setting.
- At first, allow the children to bring in any item from home. Often this will be a favourite toy. After a while change the criteria to be something related to the topic or from a birthday or holiday.
- Give four or five large zip wallets to four or five children in the group and explain that only the children with a wallet are to bring in show and tell.
- Put a laminated prompt sheet inside the wallet for parents/carers explaining the purpose and details of show and tell so they can help their child select a suitable object.
- On the specified day, allow each child with a wallet to show and tell.
- Choose the four or five different children for next time, and give out the wallets and laminated cards.

Taking it further

Put a large box or basket in a place of importance and decorate it attractively. This is the 'show and tell box', and it is where the children place their objects at the beginning of the session. Only the children who own the objects can touch them during the day, but other children can look in the box and then ask the owner of the object to show it to them. Have a special area for the children to spread out and sit on whilst they look at each other's precious items.

This is my culture

"My Mum helped me to fill in my culture wheel, and found me some photographs of our family too. I could tell my teacher all about my brothers and what we did at home, and she helped me to tell the other children too!"

Every child in your setting will have a different experience of what life is like in a family and different experiences of home. This is their culture. By asking the children to complete a culture wheel at home with their parents and carers it gives them an opportunity to share their different routines, hobbies, family photos and favourite things with adults in the setting.

Teaching tip

The children will be thrilled to look at each other's pages in the culture book. When it is full, keep it in the book trolley so that the children can refer to it. They will be fascinated by how young they look earlier in the term, or how their tastes in favourite toys have changed!

A culture wheel is simply a circle drawn onto a sheet of A4 paper that is divided into four or six sections, like a cake. Each 'slice' has a heading written on it. Some suggestions for headings include: Family, Food, Friends, Clothes, Religion, Birthdays, Traditions, Toys, Holidays, Pets.

- Buy a scrapbook, larger than A4. This will be the 'culture book'.
- Put the scrapbook and a glue stick in a zip plastic wallet.
- Create a master culture wheel and divided it into four or six slices. Write headings on each slice of the master wheel. Start simply, and choose headings which will suit your children. Photocopy it so you have one wheel for each child.
- Glue a culture wheel onto the left hand side of the first double page spread. Leave the right hand side blank. This will be for pictures and photographs related to the headings.
- Fill in the first page of the culture book with the children. Model completing the culture wheel by going through the headings and

talking out loud through your thinking, for example: [Indicating the Traditions heading] 'Now I have to write something about my traditions – that means something my family always does...well we always eat fish and chips on a Friday night – I'll write that! And we go to Grandad's house every Bonfire Night for fireworks, so that is our tradition too. Clothes...well I love wearing my blue pyjamas – I'll draw a picture of them to show what they look like.'

- Now, on the right hand side facing the culture wheel, glue in some photos of yourself; you could include photos of you when you were a baby, or a photo of a pet, or a holiday postcard, or a photo of you on a special occasion, wearing special clothes. Talk about these with the children, explaining why they were chosen.
- Give the culture book (in the zip plastic wallet) to a child, along with a laminated card explaining the principles and when to return it. Usually a week is adequate time.

Taking it further

Put the culture book inside a large plastic tub with a lid, so that the children can take home an entire 'culture box'. Ask them to add items special to them – perhaps some clothing, a toy or a favourite book. These items can then be shared alongside the wheel and photographs.

If you have a large group of children, create two separate culture books or boxes, so that all the children have a turn in half the time. Stagger the return dates, so that you have culture time twice a week.

When the culture book has been completed by the children, create a new one but with different headings on the cake slices, to gather more information.

Bonus idea

Have a culture display board and change the heading every month or so. Ask the children to bring in something from home to create the display. For example, for the title 'Food' ask them to bring in a packet or photograph of their favourite food, or a photograph of them having breakfast. Put these together attractively where the children can see them – they love to look at photographs of each other!

That's my spot!

"Some children really struggle with their spatial awareness and are easily confused when sitting in a group, for example, in assembly, P.E. or even on the carpet in the classroom. Having a 'spot' really helped George to find his place each time, stopped him rolling off under the table and kept him calmly seated!"

It can be difficult for young children to locate a place to sit when in a large group, especially on the carpet or in the hall for P.E. Having a mat or marker on the floor helps children to quickly find their place.

In some situations it is helpful for the entire group to have 'carpet places', so they can be structured into groups of emotional development, listening skills, age and friendships. This prevents fuss when the children are required to sit on the carpet.

- Have one or two sample carpet squares in different colours. Carpet shops usually discard their sample books at the end of each season; if you can procure one of these you can use them for many different things!
- Let the child pick a mat. Explain that it will always be in the same place on the carpet, and that they are to sit sensibly on it, facing the correct way.
- Before each carpet session put their mat on the floor so that they can find their place.
- The mats will also help children who find it hard to stay in one place and try to 'creep' to another. The mats give them somewhere to return to when they receive the inevitable stern look from an adult! If necessary, use reward charts and stickers to encourage children to remain seated on their mats.

Fidgeting about!

"Erin really struggled to sit still on the carpet. Despite my best efforts at seating her in a suitable position she wriggled, jiggled, stretched and rolled continuously, disturbing everyone around her. Eventually I gave her a small piece of Blu-tack to play with, and the difference was amazing! She only needed to keep her fingers busy and the rest of her body and mind stayed focused."

Young children in particular are kinaesthetic learners. They often need to move about to listen successfully or process information. There are occasions in a group where their moving around can be disruptive to the other children. By giving them a small object and 'permission' to move their fingers and hands only, they can 'be busy' without distracting others.

It is necessary to explain to the other children how this is not a 'reward', but simply a way of helping the child to listen to what others are saying. Most children will accept this without question.

- Talk to the children about how important it is to sit still and quietly when an adult is speaking.
- Explain that some children need help with this and that they might have something in their hands to hold and move about, to help them to concentrate.
- Individually, in a quiet time, ask the children to come and look at a selection of small 'fidget' toys. Include toys which stretch, pull, twist, squeeze or have an interesting texture.
- Allow the child to choose an item, and keep it in a safe place.
- Each time you require the children to sit still and listen remind those with fidget toys to fetch them.

Teaching tip

It is useful to have a range of small objects in a special box. Let the children look through the box to choose an object that will work best for them. Remember, the golden rule is: no objects should make a sound, or roll away!

What's mine is my own!

"Every time the teacher says: 'Get a whiteboard and pen', I'm always really worried that my pen won't work. Some people never put their lids on properly and so the pens dry up, and then I get left behind when I'm trying to find a new pen when she's talking. It's never my fault!"

In the early years, independence and responsibility are key skills for children to learn. This idea promotes these skills and ensures all children have access to the equipment needed before the lesson begins.

Create a set of all the equipment each child needs to participate in carpet time, phonics, number work or handwriting. By keeping the items in a 'kit', each child has what they need each time. This increases the pace of a session, and is particularly helpful in minimising low-level disruptive behaviour.

- Have a set of large, clear zip wallets, one for each child.
- Label each wallet with each child's name and distribute them to the class.
- Put a tray of A4 'whiteboards' (laminated white paper), whiteboard pens and erasing cloths (a dishcloth cut into small squares works well) in the centre of the group.
- Let each child select one of each of the three objects to make a 'kit'.
- Keep these kits in a large plastic box or tray near the area you most often work. It takes a few minutes to give these out each time but it ensures that each child has the correct equipment when necessary.
- Explain how important it is for people to look after their belongings, and demonstrate wiping the whiteboard clean, putting the lid back on the pens and zipping the wallet closed, ready for next time.

Taking it further

These kits can be further personalised for each child by adding in traceable name cards, phoneme flashcards to copy or number lines to use where appropriate. This way all these items will always be to hand when the children need them, which will improve the flow and pace of each learning session whilst also teaching the children to be responsible for their own belongings.

Who's taken my red pen, AGAIN?

"I can never find a red and black pen to mark the register. I leave them on my desk, but then they disappear before the next session!"

As the register is a legal document it is really important to use the correct colour and type of pen for the different marks. Of course, other people will need to use these pens throughout the day for writing and marking other types of work, and then they are never returned to the desk when you need them! To stop this happening, try the following simple idea.

- Take a red pen and a black pen of the same design, suitable for completing the register.
- Turn the pens end to end, so that the nib of one pen is adjacent to the end of the other pen.
- Using an elastic band, fasten the pens together around the middle.
- You should now have essentially a 'double-ended pen' – one end red, the other black.
- Wiggle the elastic band a little to allow each pen to protrude more at the nib end to make it more comfortable for writing.
- This is now your *dedicated* register pen. As it is not a particularly comfortable pen to use other than for marking the register, people will be less likely to pilfer it!

Teaching tip

Create more of these double-ended pens or pencils to support other tasks you do in the setting. Sometimes separate colours are used in 'bubble and block' marking, or for writing in home school diaries.

Pick a pencil case!

"I love choosing from the pencil case each morning, there's loads more things to write with than a boring pencil!"

Children can quickly lose interest in mark-making when they are restricted to a graphite pencil on white paper. By putting together a toolkit of interesting writing materials children can explore different effects whilst practising basic letter and number formation.

The main tenet of this idea is so important to working in early years. Children need repeated exposure to the same tasks and activities in order to learn and consolidate their skills and understanding. The trick is to keep things interesting!

Teaching tip

This is a useful 'settling-in' activity in an F2 class, when the children arrive at the beginning of a session. Put a different pencil case on each table, along with a jotter for each child. When they enter the room (either with a parent, or alone) they are to go to their table and practise handwriting with an implement of their choice. The following day put the pencil cases on different tables to ensure that all children use a range of materials.

- Collect several different pencil cases which will be attractive to the children – consider size, shape, texture and colour.
- Fill each pencil case with an exciting range of different writing implements. Include different types such as felt tip pens, highlighters, gel pens, pastels, wax crayons, pencil crayons, metallic pens and simple pencils with exciting additions such as feathers, bells, toys and springs.
- Each morning put a pencil case out on each table or in the writing area, along with some paper.
- Encourage the children to investigate the writing implements in the pencil case and try to write their name or a particular phoneme with each one.

Graffiti table

"Sometimes I just want the children to pick up a pen or a pencil of some sort and make marks! I don't want to have to keep it or mark it, just give them the opportunity to have free rein."

By covering an entire table in paper all the children can contribute to a scribble table, or graffiti table, an idea which encourages mark-making and reduces the restrictions of orientation, scale or subject.

Mark-making is a key skill requiring many different aspects of a child's development to be in tune at once. It requires physical strength, coordination, thought, memory and spatial awareness as well as consideration for those around us if mark-making alongside others.

- Using large pieces of paper (the reverse of old wallpaper is useful for this) cover an entire table top, folding the paper underneath the table edges using masking tape to secure it, as though partially wrapping a present. Ensure that the top and edges of the table are not visible.
- Put a pot of pens/pencils/chalks/any mark-making tool you like on the table.
- Explain to the children that they can write or draw *anything* they wish on the table. They may find this hard to understand, particularly that there is no 'top' and 'bottom' to the paper – children could work opposite each other if they prefer.
- The paper may be 'full' after half an hour or it may take two days. Let the children tell you when they think it's 'finished' and replace the paper.
- Display the paper with its many marks.
- If a reluctant writer has made any significant marks, cut these out for inclusion in their record file.

Taking it further

Use this idea outdoors with paints and a large easel or attach a large piece of paper to a fence and allow the children to paint anywhere on the paper. If you want to link this to a topic ask the children to paint a topic-related object such as a flower, an animal, or a fish.

Roll up, roll up!

"The children love anything on a large scale, and a roll of cheap lining paper outside is a great way to encourage reluctant writers to grab a pen or crayon and get drawing and labelling!"

Somehow children are much more willing to use pens and paper outside, as it seems to remove the formality of the activity. By providing paper on a large scale they are not restricted to controlled or fine-motor movements and can work collaboratively alongside their friends to create a large piece of work.

Taking it further

Use the work on the roll of paper as part of a topic currently studied. The large sheet is particularly good for drawing outlines of each other in a topic such as 'Ourselves'. Before the children see the roll of paper for the first time, draw the outline of child on it (select a volunteer before the session) and roll it up again. As the group unroll the paper a shape is revealed, which they can decorate by adding features and clothes. The huge amount of paper means that they can draw around each other all day long – just make sure they use wax crayon and not felt-tip, to avoid marking clothes.

To make this activity truly inclusive ensure that you provide a wide range of writing materials, particularly those which make marks satisfyingly easily such as pavement chalks.

- Buy a roll of cheap lining paper. If this is not available, pale or lightly patterned wallpaper will work just as well.
- Unroll a long section across an area of relatively flat ground and use weights like stones or books to keep it in place.
- Provide a box of markers with bold colours for the children to use on the paper.
- Leave it blank for the children to decorate by drawing and writing. Encourage them to write letter shapes in a variety of sizes and colours – can they copy their friends? Who can draw the largest 'S'?

Chalk maps

"I had a boy in my group who persistently used the wrong grip on his pencil. I had to find a wider implement for him to grip, and fat chalk sticks were perfect. The bonus was that they left a mark however they were moved across the surface, and it didn't matter if he varied the pressure. It really helped him to succeed."

Young children can find the physical aspect of writing (holding an implement at the correct angle, at the correct place on the shaft, applying the correct pressure) very challenging. By using fat chalk sticks lots of these problems are reduced and it gives them confidence to try other types of mark-making.

Try to find other activities which mimic the patterns in handwriting but which do not require a pencil and lined paper.

- Playground chalks are perfect for this activity. Outdoors, find a flat space suitable for drawing on. The children should be able to draw directly on the ground (tarmac, paving slabs, concrete etc.) but you could use large pieces of cardboard instead.
- Put a basket of small vehicles alongside the chalks.
- Model driving a car around the space. Decide whether your car will move in straight lines or if it will follow a winding route or a combination of both.
- As an example, draw a simple road for the toy cars to drive along.
- Leave this activity out for the children to investigate however they choose.
- When your focused child selects this task observe him or her closely, and help him/her to use the correct grip on the chalk.

Teaching tip

If you have a child who is persistently forming a letter shape incorrectly, for example writing 'o' clockwise instead of anti-clockwise, then this is a great way to teach the correct formation in an interesting manner. Draw an 'o' shaped track on the ground, and ask the child to repeatedly drive their toy car around it anti-clockwise, or fill 'the road' with lines of different colours.

Tidy silhouettes

"This is a really old-fashioned idea, but it really helped the children to tidy the classroom and to look for things that were lost or in the wrong place – it just shows that the old ideas can be the best!"

The key to keeping a tidy setting is not to have too much in it! Regularly take a critical look at the things you have and the way they are stored; it is tempting to harbour too much clutter.

Having a tabletop or trolley top that you use for storing objects such as scissors, pencils, crayons, glue, hole punches and sticky tape is a good way of ensuring that all the items are replaced at the end of each session.

- Arrange the objects on the tabletop in the way in which you want them to be kept.
- Draw around the base of each item on black paper.
- Cut out the shape and stick it onto the tabletop in the desired position.
- Make a simple label to put on the outline shape, but do not overlap the edges – the silhouette or 'footprint' should be clearly visible.
- At the end of each session glance at the table top – it will be immediately apparent if someone has not replaced the sticky tape dispenser!

Taking it further

Use this silhouette idea outdoors to tidy up the large equipment, or a big shelf which stores sand and water toys. If there is a 'footprint' for each item the children will want to take the equipment from the sandpit or water tray and match it to the shape – inadvertently tidying up!

Encouraging independent writing

"It can be difficult to encourage some children to write independently. I found that by creating a writing corner with a variety of sizes, colours and types of paper even the most reluctant writer would wander over to look at what was there each day. The smaller and more strangely shaped pieces of paper and card seemed to appeal particularly to the boys!"

Encourage reluctant mark makers to give it a go by providing them smaller surface areas to write on!

A4 paper can be intimidating for reluctant mark-makers. The space looks so large and white that they sometimes avoid writing altogether because they know what it *should* look like (i.e. the writing on a page in a book) but feel unable to create something which looks the same. By putting out a variety of colours and sizes of paper in the writing area children will be encouraged to write a simple word or phrase, as that is all that will fit!

- Choose a variety of coloured paper, each of a different thickness. Include tissue paper, crêpe paper, wrapping paper, paper doilies, blank cards, gift tags, Post-it notes, sticky labels etc.
- Cut this paper into small pieces and different shapes and fold some to make simple cards.
- Cut out shapes such as small squares, circles, ovals and triangles; narrow strips for writing horizontal sentences and phrases; wider strips for vertical lists of shopping or names.
- Collect a variety of different coloured pens, pencils and crayons.
- Explain to the children that they can play in the writing area at any time, and that they can make anything they like.

Taking it further

Have a writing opportunity within each role-play situation. Include the necessary equipment for the children to create appropriate resources within the theme. Examples include making name badges, invitations, maps, instructions, lists, records and price labels. Put some examples of your own into the role play to give the children ideas, and then create the blanks for them to extend their play independently.

Easy display of writing

"I find that the children write less well in their books than on interesting pieces of paper. When I hand out an unusual shape of coloured paper and explain that they are to record their ideas on it instead of in their usual book, the quality always seems to improve!"

Writing can seem repetitive to young children. By constantly varying the purpose, materials and outcome, children can be fooled into thinking they are undertaking a completely different task!

Link the topic that the children are writing about to the colour and shape of the paper they are working on. For example, if they are writing about winter weather cut out pale blue icicles or white snowballs, or simple mini-beasts, or vehicle shapes.

- Decide on the most appropriate colour and shape for the subject.
- Try to keep it very simple to avoid complicated cutting out.
- Draw lines where you want the children to write their words or phrases.
- Run the master copy through the photocopier to print onto coloured A4.
- Help the children to write their names on the front of the work, ready for display.
- The work stays neater and flatter if you cut it out after the children have written on it —if you cut out a delicate shape prior to the writing it is prone to curling up or tearing. Ensure that each child keeps their writing inside the shape as far as is possible.

Colour mixing for the squeamish!

"Some children don't like to have wet or messy hands, particularly those with autistic tendencies. This idea lets them explore and experience colour mixing whilst keeping their hands clean and dry."

Putting paint inside a malleable container such as a plastic sandwich bag allows the children to manipulate the paint inside and observe the colour changes taking place, without any mess! Squishing the paint feels fun and is an activity enjoyed by children of any age from babies to school-aged children.

Colour mixing is a favourite activity of most young children but many experiments simply end up with brown sludge. This idea helps adults to manage the colours in order to get the best effects.

- Squeeze two blobs of different coloured paint into some sealable transparent zip-lock sandwich or freezer bags and seal the top, with minimal air inside.
- Use less of the darker colour to ensure that the colour change is successful – if you use similar amounts of yellow and blue, for example, the paint will remain blue and not turn green.
- Let the children squeeze the bag to move the paint around inside, gradually mixing the colours together.
- Some children will be content when the colours begin to mix together in a marbled effect, whilst some will keep squishing until it is uniformly the secondary colour.

Taking it further

Display these bags of paint by hanging them on a washing line. To increase the effect, hang them in order of shade or border the display with the colour strips available from the paint-mixing machine at a DIY store.

Bonus idea ★

For children with additional special needs relating to muscle tone and strength, replace one of the paint colours with PVA glue. Explain to the children that they are to squish and squeeze the bag until no white glue is visible. PVA is harder to mix with paint so it will build finger strength.

Easy painty writing

"Using my fingers to write in the paint is BRILLIANT! It's so messy and it doesn't matter if you make a mistake – you just rub your hands all over it and draw it again!"

Hand or finger painting can be messy. This idea shows how children can make a painty mess all over an entire table. The lack of implements to hold also makes this task accessible for all levels of ability: babies and toddlers love it! With a more tightly defined focus it can be used for handwriting practice, writing simple words over and over to learn spellings or to investigate colour mixing and printed effects.

Teaching tip

Using a piece of paper, press it down over the marks the child has made on the black plastic. This makes a print of their work, which can be saved. The child can then use their hands to 'erase' their work on the black plastic and begin all over again!

This idea requires no paper at all, simply a bin-liner and paint. If you do not have a table it can even be done on the floor!

- Cover the top of table with a black plastic bin-liner and tape it down over the edges so that none of the table is visible.
- If you are outdoors you do not need to cover the floor, but if indoors you may also need to cover the carpet/floor surface.
- Fill a bowl with warm soapy water for children to wash their hands immediately afterwards, and a towel for drying. Do not allow the children to wander off from the painting table with paint on their hands!
- Choose two paint colours that will contrast with the black plastic surface (yellow and orange work well, as do white and metallics) and that suit your topic. Squirt the paints directly onto the plastic in the middle of the table.
- With their sleeves rolled up and clothes protected, allow the children to put their fingers and hands directly into the paint and 'draw' onto the black plastic surface.
- When the paint covers the entire area, demonstrate how children can use fingers to 'draw' by pulling and pushing their fingers

through the paint to reveal the black plastic underneath.

- When it is tidy up time, simply peel the bin-liner from the table and throw it in the bin.

If paint is too messy for your setting use dry materials in a tray in a similar manner. Fine, dry sand is a great material which children can 'draw' in with their finger. This does not require any manipulation of an implement and frees the children to focus upon the movement and orientation of the letters they are writing.

Dried tea leaves are a safe and fragrant alternative to fine sand, as is couscous or sugar. To add interest, put some cars in the tea leaves and let the children 'drive' the cars through the dry material, leaving tracks in the shape of letters.

The most successful trays I have found are those purchased at a builders' yard! Called 'Tuff Spots' or similar, they are designed for builders to mix cement on the ground. They are shallow; made from light plastic they are big enough for several children to play at once. They are useful in many ways, for example, to contain a pile of construction materials such as bricks; to create a small world; or to hold collage material so that it can be spread out without being spread all over the setting!

Taking it further

To encourage pre-writing skills, use clear plastic to cover the table and put simple shapes or letters underneath. Encourage the children to 'draw' in the paint with their fingers, tracing the shapes underneath. Include vertical and horizontal lines, zigzags, spirals and wavy lines. You could also have shapes or patterns on a laminated card for them to copy. These can then be press-printed onto paper to make a permanent record of their pre-writing achievements.

Children can practise writing their name by 'writing' it over and over again, without fear of making a permanent mistake. This method is also useful for learning phoneme patterns or spellings in a 'look, cover, write, check' manner.

Colour mixing also works really well with this idea. Squirt two primary colours onto the plastic and let the children investigate mixing the paint colours together. Make prints of their progress along the way to record the degrees of colour change.

Invisible graffiti

"The children love this idea. It is simple yet great fun, and can be done on a small or large scale depending on the outside space available. It can also be structured to suit specific learning objectives related to handwriting, letter and numeral formation and phonics."

Using a variety of brushes, the children can 'paint' outside with water. On a dry day their marks are visible, allowing them to write and draw for a short time before the marks dry.

Teaching tip

Set them a challenge linked to the maths planning for the week. For example, how many number fives can they draw in one minute, or how many triangles can they fit onto a paving slab?

Invisible graffiti is also an introduction to the effects of the sun, heating and drying. The children will all be able to talk about where puddles go after this!

- Gather together several buckets for water and a variety of brushes.
- Include brushes of different types and sizes, including wallpaper paste brushes, wide decorators' paintbrushes, fine watercolour brushes, tooth brushes, sweeping brushes, dustpan brushes and a selection of familiar paintbrushes from the classroom.
- On a dry day take the children outside and show them where they can 'paint' with the water. It may be a floor or wall surface, or a mixture of both.
- Let them investigate the effect of the water on the different surfaces.
- Allow them to paint shapes, patterns, letters and numerals with the water, or encourage them to practise writing their name or phonemes linked to the phonics programme.
- Use a digital camera to record the marks made by the children, to save as evidence of their attainment for later assessment and future target setting.

Sign up, sign up!

"To speed up the children when they are getting changed for P.E. or putting on their shoes I offer stickers to the first few children ready. This encourages the slow-coaches to hurry, and by writing their names on the board they get some extra handwriting practice too!"

For some children, getting changed at school may be the first time they have dressed independently. It is important that they practise this skill at home and at school, and this idea promotes their independence by rewarding them for effort.

To encourage the children to get changed quickly and quietly for P.E., offer a reward such as stickers for the first children ready. Depending on the size of the group, have enough stickers for just over half of the children, so a sticker is achievable but not a certainty.

- Let the children collect their kit. If you want to 'skew' the results slightly, choose the slowest dressing children to fetch their kit first and therefore give them a head start!
- Explain that when they are dressed they can have a sticker, but that there are not enough stickers for everyone so they must concentrate on being very organised at dressing themselves.
- Give out stickers for the first children changed. When they are ready have a task available for them to complete (for example reading a book) to avoid any disruption.
- If the children are older, ask them to write their names on the board in a list when they are changed. When all children are ready give stickers or a reward to the first few children on the list.
- If there are children who will never be first at dressing themselves, repeat the task for getting *undressed*, or for a simpler task at which you know they will succeed.

Teaching tip

Draw a shape, for example a flower with six petals or a car with four windows, on the whiteboard. Tell the children that the first few children changed into their kit can have their names in the petals or windows.

It's my turn next!

"I love playing in the construction area but there's always a group who get in there first and stay in there for ages! And if I go outside to play I miss the changeover time and miss my turn again!"

By having a clipboard at the edge of each of the popular play areas, children can sign up and know that they will not miss their turn when the adult announces, 'Change over time!' This also encourages all children to learn how to make their mark, even an initial, as suddenly writing has a purpose. If the adult cannot read their name on the list then they miss their turn!

- Put a clipboard with a plain sheet of paper and a pencil on a string at the entrance to each area, for example construction, sand, water, computers, role play etc.
- Explain to the children that when they go to the area and it is 'full', then they must write their name on the list, or make a mark to represent themselves.
- At regular intervals throughout the session go to the clipboard and say, 'Change over time!' and read out the next few names on the list.
- There is nothing stopping the children returning to their favourite areas over and over again during the same session as long as they are called in turn from the list.
- Some children may have changed their mind between signing up and being called to play. This is fine – just move their names down the list.
- Remember to cross off the names of the children when you have called them.

What do I need to take home?

"The end of the day causes confusion for some children. They can never remember the things that they need to gather together and as a result invariably leave something behind!"

This idea can work for either individual children or for a group of children. Photographs help them to see what belongings they need to collect and where to find them.

For most children, one class picture showing the general items they need to gather and take home is enough. However, for some individuals may need a personal guide to help them get ready.

- Take a photograph of the child wearing their coat. It is important that it is the actual child and they are wearing their own coat.
- Take a photograph of their lunchbox, water bottle and book-bag where appropriate.
- Cut out the photographs and laminate them.
- Attach Velcro to the back of each photograph, and on a separate strip of card attach the other part of the Velcro so that the photographs can be stuck on.
- Make a small box with a posting slot, decorated with characters and stickers chosen by the child in the photographs.
- Show the child how to look at the strip with the attached photographs to find out what to collect first. When they have collected it, return to the strip, pull off the appropriate photograph and post it in the box. Move onto the next photograph.
- When all photographs are gone the child should be ready to go home!

Taking it further

This idea can be used across the curriculum to help children to organise themselves in a variety of ways. For example: changing for P.E, collecting resources for beginning to write, routine of getting ready for lunch or getting ready for bed at home.

That's my job!

"The adult is always saying, 'Tidy up!' but I'm never sure what to do. Everyone is busy and I just walk around getting in the way."

To some children, the phrase 'Tidy up!' has no meaning at all. However, if each child has a specific task within the setting then they know that at 'tidy-up time' they go to that particular area and carry out the job.

Teaching tip

Make a chart for the wall with pictures showing the different roles, for example, a chart in the shape of a clock face. Put each child's name onto laminated paper and put Velcro on the back of each name. Also attach Velcro onto the clock face where the numbers would be. This way, each week you can move the names around the clock face to new roles. The clock enables the children to see what their role will be next.

Talk with the children about what the setting looks like when it is tidy, and what jobs need to be done at tidy-up time. Make a list of these things together and then let them select a job to do. Write their names at the side of each task. This could become a more permanent display if necessary. Ideas for specific tidying jobs may include:

- picking up crayons
- hanging up aprons
- putting construction away into boxes
- tucking chairs under the tables
- putting books tidily in the book trolley
- checking the cloakroom for tidiness
- tidying the home corner – separate into tasks such as putting plates and bowls in the cupboards; putting baby things in the basket; putting clothes on the rail.

Put the children into pairs to ensure that they go to the correct place in the setting to tidy together. Explain that when they are finished with their task they are to sit quietly and look at a book until the adult says that the setting is tidy.

No room!

"I love playing in the role play area but when there are lots of people in there it is a real squash! When there is a band to wear I know how many people can play there and when there is a space."

Coloured bands corresponding to each play area show how many children can play safely in which area. The easiest for children to wear and for practitioners to store are the strip bands worn diagonally across the body, as in P.E.

- Discuss with the children how many children can play safely in each area of the setting at one time.
- Make some clear notices saying how many children are allowed in, and display these clearly beside each area.
- Hang the corresponding number of coloured P.E. bands from the notices. Use different colour bands for each area, for example blue for water tray, yellow for sand, red for construction etc.
- Explain to the children that they must wear a band for each area and they also have to replace the band afterwards. If they approach the area and there are no bands hanging up, then they must come back to the area later.

Taking it further

You can use a similar system for outdoor areas, but be aware of health and safety if children are climbing and balancing. For example, to restrict the number of children on a climbing frame, use brightly coloured 'hair scrunchies' (elastic hair ties/bobbles) which the children can wear around their wrists. They are close-fitting and should not cause any child to become entangled in the apparatus.

Pass it on!

"There are many really good circle games designed to encourage focus and concentration, with the added bonus of promoting friendships!"

Sitting together in a circle and smiling quietly at each other increases the sense of calm and promotes gentleness and friendship. As with all of these circle games, if a child is too nervous or reluctant to speak in the circle they can simply 'pass' when it is their turn.

Teaching tip

If the children initially find the abstractness of passing a smile around the circle too challenging, include a soft toy. Pass this around, and smile at each other as it is given to the next child in the circle.

This is a group activity which can be done with any number of children.

- Ask the children to sit in a circle.
- To model the game, include yourself in the circle. It is important that you also sit on the floor.
- Practise smiling as a group – grin wildly and turn to look at each other's smiles.
- Explain to the children that they are to take it in turns to smile at the person next to them. When they have 'caught' the smile from the person next to them they are to turn to the person on the other side and 'pass on' the smile.
- This game requires all children to sit quietly and watch the progress of the smile around the circle. If there are children who find this difficult sit them next to an adult for support, or let them begin the game.
- When the smile returns to the sender, say 'thank you' and clap each other as a 'well done'.

Another similar idea is 'pass the squeeze'. Sitting in a circle, all the children hold hands. You begin the game by gently squeezing the hand of the child on your left. This child then squeezes the hand of the child on their left, and the squeeze is passed around the circle. It is always worthwhile talking about gentle squeezes at the beginning of the game to avoid any crushed fingers! As with the first game, when the squeeze comes back to the initiator they say 'thank you!' and everyone claps.

When the children are able to successfully pass the squeeze around the circle (and this can take some practising!) you can extend the game into a 'whodunnit'.

- Show the children how to squeeze each other's hands surreptitiously.
- Choose one child to stand in the middle of the circle.
- Explain to the child in the middle that the squeeze may start anywhere in the circle and that they are to point to, or say the name of the child doing the squeeze when they spot it.
- Ask the child standing in the centre to close their eyes.
- Point silently to a child sitting in the circle to select them to start the squeeze.
- When the squeeze is moving around the circle, tell the child standing in the centre to open their eyes and find it!
- Give them unlimited opportunities to guess where the squeeze is or limit them to three or five attempts.
- When the child in the centre correctly identifies who has the squeeze they swap with another child and the game begins again.

Use this method to introduce new children to the group. Pass a soft toy or puppet around the circle and ask the children to introduce themselves to the puppet. This reduces the fear of speaking to a large group of children. They can avoid eye contact with the group as they look at the puppet and say, 'My name is Jamie'. Passing it on to a neighbour encourages sharing and turn taking.

Listen carefully

"This is an excellent game for beginning or consolidating aural discrimination skills in order to lay the foundation for phonics and early word building."

By encouraging the children to listen carefully to everyday sounds they begin to identify the similarities and differences between them. This in turn will help when they begin to blend and segment words for reading and spelling.

Taking it further

Take photographs of the objects and make several copies on small cards. Give a card to each child. Make a sound with an object, and invite the children to stand up if they think they can hear the object on their card. Extend this idea by replacing the household objects with actual percussion instruments, and let the children explore them independently before and after the activity.

Phase One of the phonics programme has many similar listening and discriminating games. This idea uses items easily found within a setting.

- Place an easel or a board near the children, ensuring that they cannot see behind it.
- Collect a selection of objects which are familiar to the children and which also make a noise. Some examples include: a bunch of keys, a metal saucepan and lid, a teaspoon in a mug, a cup and saucer, a mobile phone ringtone or a noisy toy from the setting.
- Without the children seeing, select an object and make a noise with it behind the screen.
- Ask the children to identify the sound they can hear. To make this easier you could let them investigate the objects beforehand and explore their properties.
- When a child correctly identifies an object let them come and stand behind the screen to make a sound of their own choosing.

Shadow maps

"Map work and the concept of plan view can be difficult for young children to grasp. By looking at familiar objects in both real-life and plan view as a shadow, the children can begin to make links between the two."

Children can find the abstractness of plan view confusing. This idea lets them hold a familiar object and then explore how it could look from different perspectives.

There is a little setting up required before the children enter the room. The key thing is not to allow the children to see any of the objects before the game begins!

- Set up an overhead projector (OHP) and display screen.
- Attach a piece of card to the edge of the light box of the OHP so that the children sitting on the floor cannot see any objects sitting on the glass of the light box, only the display screen.
- Put a pair of scissors onto the light box and turn it on.
- The shadow of the scissors will be clearly projected onto the large screen, and the children will be able to identify them immediately.
- Explore other objects with the children. Include easily identifiable objects such as a paperclip, glove, cutlery, clothes peg and comb, alongside more challenging ones such as a pen, dice, sharpener, tin can and toilet roll tube. Some objects can be very difficult to identify from certain angles and are revealed when turned around to a different position. A wooden clothes peg laid on one side is simply a rectangle. When turned over onto another side it has a distinctive shape.

Teaching tip

Make some outline shadow cards and group them in a basket with the actual objects. Encourage the children to pair the objects. Include the light box in the display if it makes it more fun!

Coordinating coordinates!

"Children love the idea of buried treasure. This idea gives them a first experience of coordinates on a very simple, practical scale."

By creating a real-life small world in the sand tray the children are able to bury treasure and then use simple coordinates to direct their friends to find it.

- Put a 5-10cm layer of sand in a large sand tray.
- Attach three pieces of string over the edges, to make a physical grid as follows: one piece of string the length of the tray, and two shorter pieces over the width. This will divide the tray into six sections.
- Bury small toys – 'treasure' – in the sand.
- Using stickers on the side of the tray, label each section A1, A2, A3, B1, B2, B3 as in a grid reference system and make a note for yourself which treasure is hidden where.
- Explain to the children how to count along and up the squares to find the correctly numbered square.
- Guide the children to the toy by saying the coordinate of the square where the treasure is hidden.
- Let the children play at hiding and then finding the treasure with their friends.

To extend and consolidate their knowledge of maps and coordinates, make it into a dice game. Allow the children to play in pairs, rolling the dice to select the square to search.

- Have a dice numbered only 1, 2, and 3.
- Have another dice labelled A and B.
- Show the children how to roll both dice to generate the coordinate of a square.
- Take it in turns to roll the dice and dig in a square until the treasure is found.

Bonus idea ★

Use smaller trays in groups of three or four children to enable them to create their own 3D maps. If they can 'walk' a small toy character around their map it will bring it to life!

- As a group, talk about the environment they wish to create.
- Use sand, compost, paper, gravel, a selection of construction toys, small world toys, toy cars and natural materials to build a landscape in the tray.
- Help them to make the string grids over the trays. Simplify them into only four squares if necessary.
- Ask the children questions about their 3D map – what is in each square? Can they add extra features?

Amateur archaeologists

"It is so exciting when you don't know what you are going to find buried in the ice. It's difficult to get it out with just the tools but I love doing it!"

Children love surprises. By hiding different objects in blocks of ice the children have to be patient and work as a team to discover what is inside.

This idea needs time to prepare and for the ice to freeze. Ensure that you have a freezer large enough to hold the containers!

- Collect some large plastic containers of different shapes. Examples include ice-cream tubs, two litre drinks bottles cut open lengthways, four-pint milk bottles cut in half, butter tubs and jelly moulds.
- 'Hide' small objects in the ice, for example, small toy soldiers, Lego bricks, small construction, shells, pebbles, small dolls' clothes, small plastic toys, pegs, counters, marbles and plastic magnetic letters and numbers – by putting a handful of the items into a container and fill it with water.
- Put the container in the freezer. Large containers will take a while to freeze completely, so prepare them in plenty of time.
- Put the large chunk of ice containing the objects into the water tray.
- Provide a selection of wooden tools for the children to safely 'dig' the ice block.
- Eye protection (sunglasses), gloves and aprons may be useful.

Teaching tip

If the objects are floating to the top of the container when you fill it with water, try to weigh them down with a handful of ice cubes or freeze shallow layers of water one after the other, placing a different object in each layer.

Bonus idea ★

Bury the numerals 0 to 10 in the ice block. The aim of the activity is for the children to chip out all the numbers and to place them in order. This idea can be used across other curriculum areas, including phonics (group the rhyming phonemes/order the letters), science (group materials by their properties), maths (group the shapes with curved sides). The permutations are endless!

Iceberg ahoy!

"This is a really simple idea, but it works equally well indoors or outdoors, in summer or winter, and costs nothing! Children are familiar with ice and love exploring its properties."

Children will enjoy playing with the different shaped icebergs and watching them melt. By putting them in the water tray they can not only observe them melting but also measure how quickly they melt or look at how they float and sink in water.

Try to collect interestingly shaped containers for this idea. Food packaging often comes in unique shapes and is completely free!

- Fill a variety of containers of different sizes and shapes with water. Include containers such as drinks bottles, balloons, ridged plastic cups, ice cream tubs and latex gloves. Many of these items can be cut from around the frozen ice and thrown away.
- Put the containers into a freezer to freeze until solid.
- Remove the ice shapes from the containers (for example cut away the latex glove, leaving an iceberg in the shape of a hand) and put them in the empty water tray.
- Add water to the tray if you are looking at floating and sinking – mixing food colouring into the water makes the ice shapes more noticeable. Aprons to protect clothing are advised!
- Add glitter or food colouring to the ice moulds if you want to make the lumps of ice more interesting.

Taking it further

Have some salt available for the children to pour onto the ice lumps. Look at how the salt rapidly melts the ice, and listen to hear if it makes a crackling sound. Talk with the children about the use of salt and grit to make slippery surfaces safe in the winter.

Stained ice windows

"Although this art activity is messy it is great fun and each child can create something completely unique. No skill is needed, and everyone can achieve success!"

By freezing coloured strips of tissue paper in a shallow tray, each child or a group of children can create a 'stained glass window' made from ice. Photograph it quickly though, before it melts!

This idea takes more than one session to complete, as it involves preparing shallow ice trays before adding the tissue paper, and freezing again at the end. Prepare two or three days to complete the entire idea.

- Gather together some shallow trays, around A5 size. Take-away food containers work well, particularly transparent plastic ones with lids.
- Put a thin layer of water in each tray and freeze it.
- Meanwhile, tear different coloured tissue paper into narrow strips.
- Show the children how to lay the strips along the ice in the bottom of the tray, overlapping some to create different colours.
- Gently pour more water onto the strips and place the tray back into the freezer.
- When it is a solid lump, take the ice sheet from the tray (it should come out easily) and let the children hold it up to the light to investigate the colours.
- Lay the ice sheets out like a tiled pattern, to look at them all together. This is best done outside – the coloured tissue paper can stain fingers, fabric and flooring.
- Photograph them quickly before they melt!

Taking it further

These can be replicated indoors in a clean, dry way using tissue paper and a laminator. Give each child a piece of laminating pouch. Show them how to tear strips of tissue paper and lay them inside the laminating pouch, overlapping to create different colours. Laminate the pouch to create a 'stained glass' effect. By cutting the pouch into a bookmark shape, and finishing them with a hole-punch and ribbon tied in a tassel at the bottom, the children can make bookmarks as presents or for a stall at a school fair.

Marshmallow igloos

"This idea combines sweets and construction – what a winning combination. And the best bit is that you can eat the igloo at the end!"

Igloos are fascinating to children but can be difficult to create from ice cubes as they melt so quickly with the heat from the children's hands. By using marshmallows there is no preparation needed to cut the blocks to size, and they are sticky without melting.

Ensure that no one in the setting is allergic to any of the ingredients in marshmallows before beginning this idea. If they are, their parents or carers may be able to offer an alternative product.

- Buy a bag of white marshmallows. They are available in different sizes. You will probably need more than one bag to build a single igloo.
- Put some fresh water and a new paintbrush into a mug.
- Show the children a picture of an actual igloo. Talk about the shape of the blocks and the dome construction.
- Encourage the children to wash their hands before handling the marshmallows (if they are to eat them afterwards).
- Demonstrate to the children how to moisten the paintbrush with water and wet the edge of the marshmallow. When the marshmallows are wet they will become sticky and join together.
- A word of warning – too much water will cause the marshmallows to slide and not stick to each other. Less is more!
- Let the children play with the marshmallows, attempting to build walls and domes.

Cereal castles

"The children love building with breakfast cereals. There are so many different types and shapes that they can create extravagant designs, and then glue them down to keep!"

By using a selection of differently shaped breakfast cereals the children can work together as a group to design a detailed building such as a castle. There are many different sizes and shapes of cereals, and the collaborative team approach encourages children to talk about shape and size and to justify their choices.

Depending on the theme of the construction you may choose more of one type of cereal. For example, if you are making vehicles ensure you have enough circles for wheels.

- Gather a selection of breakfast cereals. Include large oval or rectangular biscuit type cereals: hoops, shapes, woven squares and flakes of different colours.
- Lay a large piece of card on the floor or a table top.
- Have a selection of pictures and photographs of different buildings for the children to look at for inspiration.
- Encourage the children to work in pairs to create their castle. Tell them to use as many shapes as they need and to arrange the cereal pieces on the paper.
- When they have finished their castles they could glue down the shapes to create a permanent picture, or they could take a photograph of their creation and the cereal pieces can be used again by another group.

Teaching tip

This type of collage activity could be replicated using many other types of food. Dried pasta is an obvious one, as are dried pulses, beans or biscuits! Instead of castles, countryside scenes work well with pasta and pulses, and biscuits of different shapes make super vehicles due to the large variety of circular 'wheels'!

Sliding shapes

"I love playing this game. We wait to see what is going to pop out and all shout out the name of the shape."

This idea is a great lesson starter or a plenary. By hiding a selection of shapes out of sight and then slowly revealing one, the children are forced to recall the properties of familiar shapes and apply what they know to identify and name them.

Taking it further

Put the shapes inside a drawstring cloth bag, or 'feely bag'. The children put one hand inside the bag and describe the shape they can feel by using mathematical language to describe it, for example, 'It's got some corners', 'I can feel a curve'.

Bonus idea ★

This idea works brilliantly with large wooden letters as part of a handwriting session or numerals as a numeracy starter. Introduce a small selection of letters to the children – they may be linked to your phonics programme for that week. Model the correct formation of the letters on the board before sliding up one of the wooden letters for them to identify.

This idea is very popular when played by the children themselves. When you have finished demonstrating it to the class allow the children to play it independently, as it will extend their vocabulary and mathematical language.

- Ask the children to sit on the floor in front of an easel or board.
- Seat yourself to the side so that you have access to the back of the board but so that you can also see the children on the floor.
- Select a large 2D shape without the children seeing it, and hide it behind the board.
- Slowly slide the shape up the back of the board so that an edge of the shape begins to peep over the top becoming visible to the children.
- Before revealing the whole shape, stop and ask the children to guess what shape it might be – does it have a point? Is it curved?
- At this point they could cross off the impossible shapes from a laminated sheet, or draw the possible shapes onto a small whiteboard.
- The child who identifies the shape correctly gets to come behind the board and select the next shape.

What am I?

"This is a great opening activity to a new topic. It works for many subject areas and is transferable across the curriculum. I found that my class grasped the idea very quickly and were delighted when this game popped up again in a different subject."

Find an artefact linked to the new topic that the children can hold and explore. Through observing, asking and answering questions the class can help a blindfolded child to identify what it is that they are holding.

The success of this game can depend entirely upon the nature and ability of the child holding the object, so choose carefully!

- Select a child from the group to sit at the front, wearing a blindfold.
- Ensure that the blindfolded child is capable of asking questions and understanding answers.
- Explain that whilst they are blindfolded the other children are going to look at an artefact and try to help them identify it through questioning.
- Give the blindfolded child the artefact to hold. Remind the children in the audience not to shout out what it is and spoil the surprise!
- Model a question to help the children understand the game, for example, 'Is it something you wear?'
- Encourage lots of questions, choosing different children from the group to answer the questioner.
- When the artefact is identified correctly, remove the blindfold.

Teaching tip

Artefacts could include: objects with significance to a particular religion; puppets from a story or rhyme; a costume worn by a particular character; a number card (encourage the children to ask questions about the number using greater than and fewer than); a piece of scientific equipment; any natural materials; a picture linked to the topic.

Taking it further

Use this idea as a starter activity at the beginning of the session. Put out an object where it is visible to the whole class. Ask them to think of questions to ask about the item, or statements of fact about it. Where appropriate, write these on whiteboards or work in groups with an adult as scribe.

Washing line pictures

"Children love pegging things on washing lines. The non-permanence of the outcome encourages all children to 'have a go'."

By providing the children with large, laminated colour pictures they can explore and investigate a topic before beginning to study it. The open-ended nature of the task means that all the children can participate at a level appropriate to them.

Although this idea is included here as an early years activity, it can also be used to great effect with older children in Key Stages One, Two and even Three.

- Collect large pictures and photographs linked to the new topic.
- Laminate them so that they are resilient to lots of handling.
- Put up a washing line, with clothes pegs attached, at a height appropriate to the children taking part in the activity.
- Explain to the children that they are going to look at the pictures and photographs and sort them however they like. Discuss what 'sort' might mean – group together similar colours; sizes; black and white pictures; animal pictures; pictures of people etc.
- Observe the children as they sort and group. It is the process of sorting and the language used in their justification which will inform your assessment for learning.
- When the children have sorted the photographs, look at them together and encourage them to talk and explain their choices and reasoning to the rest of the group.

Bonus idea ★

Use actual objects to group on the washing line. This idea works well for religious or historical artefacts, or those which introduce another culture. If they are not suitable to peg on a washing line, use a skipping rope stretched out on the floor as a kind of 'flat' line, or some large hoops for grouping the objects.

Which one am I?

"I didn't know that there were so many different kinds of gloves! My friends and I tried them all on and then decided which ones went together".

This is a similar activity to 'Washing line pictures', except that here the children are able to handle and try on items which are familiar to them. This engages early years children much more.

Collect many different types of the same object, for example footwear, gloves or headwear. By having a variety the children are required to look carefully at what is the same and what is different, and to use descriptive language to assess each one before grouping them.

- Collect a set of objects, for example gloves. Include as many different types as possible, such as woollen mittens, baby scratch mitts, ski gloves, oven gloves, gardening gloves, rubber washing up gloves, welding gauntlets, latex medical gloves, stretchy wool gloves, cricket gloves, motorcycle gloves etc.
- Put them into a basket for the children to look at. Encourage them to try each one on!
- Model language when you are looking at them together, using language of size, material properties and descriptive touch.
- Put out some sorting hoops for the children to group the items. Ask them how they have chosen their criteria, encouraging them to verbalise and justify their choices.

Taking it further

Have some photographs of people at different stages in their lives, or dressed as different professions. Encourage the children to pair each picture and object, for example a baby and the scratch mitts; a ski or snowboard athlete and the ski gloves. Are there any which are ambiguous, for example gardening gloves and a man and woman of different ages? Use these to challenge the children's preconceptions and stereotypes.

It's all in the detail!

"There is so much that can be gathered from a single painting that it can be too much to look at at once! This idea allows the adult to select which aspect the children should focus on, guiding their observations".

Children can be encouraged to focus on the details in a painting or artwork by allowing them only to look at a small part of it at first, before drawing back and observing the whole.

Teaching tip

'Take One Picture' is the National Gallery's countrywide scheme for primary schools. Each year the gallery focuses on one painting from the collection to inspire cross-curricular work in primary classrooms. The challenge is then for schools to use the image imaginatively in the classroom, both as a stimulus for artwork, and for work in more unexpected curriculum areas. National Gallery Education then displays a selection of the work in the annual 'Take One Picture' exhibition at the National Gallery, and on their website. The website has a list of pictures which have been used in previous years and has lots of resources to support teaching and learning.

- Select a picture for the children to study. It may be a picture related to the topic, or part of a focus upon an artist's wider body of work.
- Make a screen for the picture so that only a small part is revealed to the children. This can be done either physically by cutting a hole in a piece of card which is larger than the picture and holding it in front of it, or by using the 'spotlight' tool on an interactive whiteboard. This allows the user to hover over a certain part of the picture and zoom outwards, revealing more of the image.
- Show the children the small part of the picture. Together, talk about what they can see, which colours are used, what they think it is and what they think may be in the rest of the picture.
- Slowly reveal the remaining pieces of the picture to tell the entire story. The 'revealing' does not have to be completed in the first session if you want the children to really focus on what they can see and use this as a basis for their artwork.
- Try to use a picture or painting with a subject matter that is relevant to the children. Views of landscape, coast, boats and sea, people in family groups and animals will have some significance to most children's lives.

- To make it more of a surprise, choose a picture with a twist. For example, if the first small porthole shows a boat on the sea then the children may assume it is a painting of a beach. It is only on the zoom backwards when more of the picture is revealed that they discover the boat is only part of a tiny view from the window of a room.
- Select an object from the picture and use this across the curriculum. Make links to geography, history, design technology, music and science particularly. Create the object through malleable materials or box modelling, and display these in the setting.

Bonus idea ★

Hold a photography exhibition. Let the children use digital cameras to take photographs of the details around them, after first using the small card viewfinders (see 'Taking it further') to find the images they like. Print these out as enlarged pictures so that it is not immediately apparent what the image is. You could pair these images with a photograph of the real object for the children or audience to match up on a display.

Taking it further

Make small postcard sized viewfinders (cut a hole in a piece of card) for the children to use around the setting. Let them search for interesting parts of the area around them, really focussing on the details they like. It may be the screws in the hinge of the door, the joins in the flooring, the lines in the fence panel or the wheels on the toy cars. Provide clipboards and pencils for the children to record what they see. Show them how to place their postcard viewfinder onto the clipboard, draw around it and the hole. Demonstrate copying the detail they admire (for example screws in the hinge) into the space on their drawing. This technique creates a frame for easy display of the work.

Hear it, draw it

"I could hear the seagulls and the music sounded like the fair. I drew a rollercoaster and some balloons because it sounded like a party".

Children are influenced by all their senses and can find it difficult to isolate only one, particularly hearing. This idea removes the temptation to use their sight when listening to film or television programme music and requires them to draw imaginatively instead.

- Select a piece of film, cartoon or television programme without spoken voices, only music.
- Set it up to play to the children, but cover or hide the screen so that they can only hear it, not see any visuals.
- Explain to the children that they are going to listen to the music and then draw pictures, shapes and patterns to reflect what they can hear.
- There may also be sound effects in the music (seagulls, doors closing, footsteps etc.) which will give clues to the subject matter and location.
- Give the children large pieces of paper to draw on.
- If you have some children who are reluctant to put pencil to paper let them work with a partner on a larger A3 piece of paper.
- Share the drawings and children's thoughts together at the end.
- If you wish, you can show the visuals to the children at the end as part of the discussion around what they could hear – some children will want to know if they were 'correct'!

Taking it further

Put out the instruments for the children to investigate, alongside some pictures to act as a stimulus. For example, they could be photographs of the weather or a landscape with animals.

Eat the alphabet

"Children are very easily motivated by food. It was amazing how their concentration and participation improved when I provided a selection of snacks which they could eat after they had ordered it alphabetically!"

Ordering pictures and objects can be boring. By introducing snack food that the children can eat afterwards you can show them how to make an alphabet on their plate, how to label each initial sound and then they can eat it afterwards!

Paper plates are an excellent tool for recording children's emergent writing. They do not appear as threatening as a piece of blank paper. In this idea they are used both as a plate and a notepad!

- Give each child a paper plate and a pencil.
- Put some dishes of food on the table, trying to use items which begin with clearly identifiable initial sounds.
- Ensure that each piece of food can be eaten with their fingers.
- Examples of suitable food include: apple pieces, banana slices, biscuits, breadsticks, carrot sticks, cheese, crackers, dips, dried fruit, scrambled egg, small chocolate eggs, flapjack, fruit, etc.
- The children can either select a letter and fill their plate with a sample of everything beginning with that letter, or make a section of the alphabet.
- Provide alphabet strips for the children to refer to as they select and eat the food.
- Ensure the children can say the names of each item, and help them to write the initial sounds on their paper plate.
- Let them eat their alphabet!

Teaching tip

Make sure you check for allergies and cultural differences and make provision for any children who cannot eat particular foods.

Taking it further

Play 'snack-time bingo'. Give each child four or five very small pieces of different foods. Draw an initial letter from a feely bag and ask the children to eat something on their plate which begins with this letter. The first empty plate is the winner!

Waiter, waiter!

"I love being the waiter at snack time. It's a really important job, and you have to wear a special hat and apron. I make sure that everyone says thank you too, or I don't let them have a snack."

All children love responsibility. This idea lets each child work with a partner to share out food and drinks at snack time, emphasising teamwork and manners.

Many activities are improved by adding an item of costume to wear. A simple card band stapled at the back with an emblem drawn or stuck on the front is enough to delineate a role. Chef's hats can easily be created by adding white crepe paper in a puffy shape inside the band.

- Obtain two aprons and two caps for the 'waiters' to wear.
- Show the children some photographs of waiters in uniform. Talk about the purpose of the special clothing – to protect clothing and to prevent the spread of germs.
- Explain to the children that at snack time they will be served by the waiters.
- Have a rota so that the children understand that they will each have a turn at being a waiter.
- Help the waiters to prepare a snack and a drink by placing it on trays that they can carry around to the other children.
- Emphasise the language used – (if there is a choice) waiters questioning, 'What would you like?', 'Would you like a drink of water?' and the customers replying, 'Yes please', 'Thank you' in a clear voice with good manners.
- If necessary, the waiters will also be involved in tidying away.

Taking it further

Involve the children in creating a menu for snacks at snack time. These could include healthy finger food such as crackers and cheese as well as more traditional foods like fruit and bread. At the beginning of each session display the menu and highlight the snack for that day.

Hard hat helpers

"In our setting the only male role model is the site manager, (or caretaker). To inspire the boys I asked him to come in and present them with a problem to solve – they absolutely loved it!"

This idea means that you can work with the caretaker to set up a practical scenario that the children can be involved in, using skills such as measuring, recording and collecting data. By providing high visibility waistcoats and hard hats the children really take the role to heart.

Speak to your caretaker, site manager or cleaner first to warn them what you intend to do. There may be an actual problem that requires a solution, or it may require a little creative thinking to come up with one.

- Select a 'problem' that the caretaker requires help with. This could be something simple like replacing the doormats, or more complex such as replacing all the hinges on the doors.
- Provide a box with hard hats, high visibility waistcoats, clipboards, paper and pencils.
- Invite the caretaker to come in and explain what he needs to do and how he needs the children's help.
- Let the children work independently to 'solve' the problem.
- Show them where the clipboards are and explain that they will need to record their answers as they go along, so that they can provide feedback to the caretaker at the end of the week.
- Save these samples of emergent writing and numbers as examples for their record file.

> **Teaching tip**
>
> Widen this idea to include other people in the setting, such as the kitchen, office or gardening staff. There are many 'problems' that the children can help with, and these problems can easily be linked to a topic currently studied by the children, or a subject such as measuring in maths.

Traffic lights

"Sometimes the teacher explains things and I don't really understand what she means, but I'm too scared to put my hand up to tell her."

Assessment for Learning is a key part of any outstanding teaching. By allowing each child to show their level of understanding using a colour card you can quickly see how many children in the group need a little extra explanation, and who is confident to work independently.

Teaching tip

If the children are too young to demonstrate their understanding using traffic light cards, simply ask them to show you a thumbs up, or thumbs down. They can also put their thumbs sideways if they are partly clear about the task. You may find that the children improvise and add their own actions, for example two thumbs high above their head when they really understand!

A key tenet of outstanding teaching and learning is understanding when to consolidate a new skill and when to move on to cover new ground. This idea enables you to quickly assess which direction to take and who needs extra support.

- Laminate two small pieces of coloured card – red and green – back to back. Each side is a 'traffic light'. Make one for each child.
- Explain to the children that at regular points throughout the discussion you will ask them if they understand what you are talking about and that they should use the traffic lights to tell you.
- Make a link with traffic lights – red for stop (or no), and green for go (or yes).
- Practise several times with simple questions to ensure that the children understand how to use the cards.
- When you are teaching, ask the children to show their cards to check understanding.

Show me, show me!

"I often use this as a quick mental or oral starter. By using their fingers it allows the children to all be involved in the starter at once, and wakes up their brains by asking them to move!"

It can be difficult for young children to use whiteboards and pens in order to answer questions on the carpet. Using their fingers enables them to work out answers accurately and show the adult that they understand the questions.

As well as it being a good mental starter to wake up their brains, the kinaesthetic nature of this activity reaches all children.

- Ask the children to hold up their hands and wiggle their fingers. Then, ask them to clap several times and rub their hands together – to rub all the 'numbers' off.
- Ask the children to hold up the matching number of fingers when you call out a number (under ten).
- Encourage them to work quickly – say the different numbers at increasing speed to make them focus and work quickly.
- Show them simple ways to find some numbers so that they do not always start counting at 'one'. For example, five is always all the fingers on one hand; nine is all their fingers minus one.
- As they get better at this, ask them to show you five 'in another way', such as showing three fingers on one hand and two on another. This encourages them to investigate the properties of each number and number bonds within these.
- Discuss the different ways chosen by each child to show the numbers.
- 'Rub' all the numbers off, then continue with different types of 'show me' such as doubles to ten or number bonds to ten.

Taking it further

Give each child a fan of numbers so that they can hold up the correct numeral for the answer. By making your own fans (laminate each card, hole punch the cards at the corners and thread string through the holes to form a loop) you can give the children particular sets of numbers such as odd or even, or multiplication tables to support the current topic.

Hold it up!

"Ofsted judge a lesson very quickly, often during the first five minutes. At our school, we found that when all the children had a small whiteboard to record their thinking and were able to be involved in the questioning and answering right from the very first minute it transformed the lesson from 'good' to 'outstanding'."

By giving each child a whiteboard and pen at the beginning of the starter or plenary they can each be involved in answering the questions posed by the adult. There is nothing worse than seeing 29 children sitting idle whilst one replies to a question!

Teaching tip

This is an excellent example of Assessment for Learning. To increase the participation of all children, particularly those with less confidence or ability, pair them with a more confident child (see also page 70 'Response partners'). This can also be done with children who are unable to use a whiteboard to record their answers, or with a special need. Children can also be paired with an adult helper to really ensure their understanding and participation.

Small whiteboards are an excellent tool for use in the setting. If the cost of them is too prohibitive then laminated photocopy paper works almost as well, costs very little and can be replaced when necessary. Dish cloths cut up into small pieces make excellent erasers.

- Ensure each child has a whiteboard at the beginning of the learning period. This idea can take place at the beginning, middle or end of the session.
- Explain to the children that they need to write their answers or ideas on the whiteboard and wait until the teacher says, "Now...show me!"
- The teacher can scan the group and look for incorrect answers, immediately assessing for learning.
- Children can work in pairs where relevant or with an additional adult if necessary.
- Provide coloured boards and pens for children with an additional need or for those with dyslexic tendencies.

Hungry Zippy

"I love Zippy. He's always hungry and it makes me laugh when he eats all the cubes from the teacher's fingers. It's really funny!"

Subtraction can be difficult for some children to understand. A hungry puppet that 'eats' cubes makes an abstract topic much easier to visualise, and as a bonus there are cubes in the mouth of the puppet for the children to count to check their answers.

- Buy a hand puppet with a large mouth. Zippy is a favourite, as is the Cookie Monster, but there are many to choose from.
- Tell the children that the puppet has come to help with their maths work. Explain that the puppet is very bad at maths and is also very hungry!
- Find some counting apparatus, for example Unifix® cubes that the children can balance on their fingers like Hula Hoop crisps.
- Choose a child to come out to the front and to hold up one hand with an open palm and fingers splayed as in a 'high five'. Put some cubes on each of their fingers, count the cubes and write the number '5' on the board.
- When you are half turned round writing on the board (or 'distracted' by something else) let the puppet gobble a cube from the child's finger.
- Look surprised – say that you thought there were five cubes on their hand, not four! Write the number '4' on the board.
- Ask the children how many cubes they think the puppet ate – look at the 'empty' finger and write the number '1' on the board.
- Check the final answer by opening the puppet's mouth and retrieving the cubes. Play this game in different permutations to explore numbers and number bonds to ten.

Teaching tip

If the children have their own number string of five or ten beads, allow them to work out the answer themselves and hold up the string to share their answer. Extend this by asking them to record their answers and number sentences on individual whiteboards to share.

Clever Cow

"If I want the children to really listen to what I am going to say I always use a puppet. I have a cow puppet we call 'Clever Cow' – the irony being that she is not clever at all and always gets the answers wrong – the children love it and howl with laughter!"

Puppets transfix all children. If used skilfully, a puppet can quickly become part of the group and can be used to help in all lessons and situations. The puppet can be any animal, it doesn't have to be a cow!

Teaching tip

Working as the puppet's 'spokesperson' is key, so make the puppet 'whisper' in your ear a lot. Turn to face the puppet and hold an imaginary secret conversation, with a lot of, 'I know! Oh, I don't think so. Do you think they (the children) will know that? Well, I could ask them. Are you sure? Oh, all right then, I will', before looking back at the children and asking your question. They will be putty in your hands!

If you enjoy using puppets, have a small collection of them available to support different activities and subjects. Change the puppet according to the nature of the topic or the interests of the children.

- Explain to the children that you have a helper with you for the day and that they are going to help with the lesson.
- Introduce the puppet by name.
- Make the puppet whisper in your ear and reply with comments like, 'Of course you can help! I know you are good at counting/reading/spelling.'
- Ask the puppet a question. Make the puppet answer in a silly voice with the *wrong* answer.
- When the children laugh, say something like, 'Oh, isn't that right? What is the answer then?'
- Continue in this vein, encouraging the children to ask the puppet questions and other children to check if the puppet's answers were correct.

Clock watching

"Learning to tell the time is very complex and takes the children a long time. I begin in the Foundation Stage by putting a clock in each room and one outside for the staff to look at and refer the children to whilst they are playing."

This may seem obvious, but as with many ideas the simplest are the best. If the children are familiar with looking at a traditional clock face with numbers they will begin to see how the time is measured and read, and they will use it in their play.

Ensure that the setting has a clock with clear numerals and large hands. Remember to put it low down on the wall so the children can see it and use it easily.

- Look around the setting from the height of the children in your group – what can they see? Can they actually see the clock?
- Have the same clock in different parts of the setting so that the children become really familiar with it.
- During taught sessions and investigation time, refer to the clock when you are talking about what the time is, what time the next activity is, minutes, hours and the end of the day.
- Sit quietly and watch the clock move round for one minute.
- Situate the clock with an interactive display of sand timers, clocks, watches and stopwatches for the children to explore and use in their play.

Taking it further

Make some wipeable clock faces and display these around the setting. Draw on the clock hands to show the children when it is tidy up time, playtime or lunchtime. Encourage them to compare the wipeable clock face with the actual clock face to check the passage of time.

Trust me, tell me

"I love playing this game. It's best in the hall where there's lots of space, and when we play in teams everyone gets really excited because we all want to win!"

By working in pairs, with one child blindfolded and the other acting as a guide, the children have to really think and use directional language carefully and accurately in order to guide their partner through an obstacle course.

This simple obstacle course can be created from just a chair across the other side of the room – no crawling or climbing is necessary.

Taking it further

Divide the children into small teams. Ask the teams to line up at the start of the obstacles. Each team should have their own course. The person at the front of the line is blindfolded, and they are directed around the course by the second person in the line. When they have completed the course they return to the back of the line and the child who has been directing (second in line) becomes the blindfolded whilst the third child becomes the director. The roles pass down the line in this way until all children have had a turn at being blindfolded. It can become a timed team race.

- Take the children into a large space – use the gym, a big hall or take the children outside, preferably to a grassy area.
- Construct an obstacle course for the children to walk around. This can be as simple or elaborate as you choose.
- Initially, begin with three chairs in a staggered line.
- Explain that they have to make their way around the chairs but can only walk in straight lines, so their instructions need to be very clear.
- When they get to the last chair or the end of the course, they are allowed to take their blindfold off and return to their team.
- Demonstrate the terms 'forwards' and 'sideways', and if appropriate 'left' and 'right'.
- Show them how to direct someone through the course, explaining what decisions you are making and why you are choosing those directions.

I can read that!

"When we do shared reading and writing I can read about loads of things from the shops. I love seeing what the teacher has bought today."

Guided reading can be challenging for young children or for those with low literacy skills. Using environmental print allows all children to 'read' and be successful – show me a child who cannot read 'M' and 'McDonalds'!

This idea can become a more permanent feature in the room by building it in as part of a wall display. Use it to great effect in other places too such as the dining hall or assembly hall.

- Gather together a selection of environmental print. Make this relevant to the area the children live in – there is no point in collecting plastic bags from a particular supermarket if the families all shop in a different one closer to their homes!
- Collect empty bags of crisps, sweet wrappings, biscuit packets and fast food boxes. Although this is in opposition to a healthy eating message, it is popular with children and they will probably have encountered the packaging before. Besides, apples don't come in a branded bag!
- Sit in a small group with the children. Tell them that you have been shopping today and that you are going to ask them to read the labels on the items you have bought.
- Share the items from your shopping bag and read the words together. Look for phonemes they recognise.
- If they are able, extend the activity to practise letter formation and handwriting on a whiteboard, based upon the words shared in the setting.

Teaching tip

Include labels and environmental print in each area of the setting. Use packaging, posters, cards and maps in areas such as the role play, construction, ICT, outdoors and in the dining hall. Remember to put the text low down so the children can see it and read it!

Taking it further

Extend the idea by asking children to group or sort the bags, labels and packaging according to the initial sound or vowel phoneme used. Make a display of their findings.

Noise slider

"One of the things I find difficult about working in early years is the noise. The children all talk so loudly that I think they forget what an 'inside voice' actually is!"

It can be difficult for young children to appreciate how noisy they are being and to understand the cumulative effect on volume of many children playing together. Using a visual prompt in this way helps them to regulate the volume of their voices.

- Draw a horizontal line on the board. Write the number '0' at one end and '10' at the other.
- Explain to the children that this is a 'noise controller', and that you are going to try it out today.
- Point to '0', and ask the children to sit in silence. Explain that this is a level without noise, called 'silence'.
- Now move up to '1' and ask the children to whisper very quietly to each other.
- Explain that '10' is the noisiest when they are outside running about playing in the playground – if you value your ears do not ask for a demonstration of this!
- Tell the children that you do not want any noise in the session louder than '4' or '5'. Write these numbers on the line, so that they can see the level.
- During the session, if they become much noisier than this bring them back to the line on the board and ask what number they think they were, and remind them to stay at '4'.

Taking it further

Incorporate the traffic lights idea here (Idea 54) to display to the children the volume you expect them to make at any one time. Cut out three circles from coloured card – red, amber and green. Label the coloured circles to describe the noise level required – red is 'silence', amber is 'quiet voices to a partner', green is 'class discussion'. Display one of these circles at the beginning of each activity and refer the children to it throughout the session.

Counting sounds

"This makes the children listen really hard and concentrate. It is much more difficult than counting visible objects, and really stretches them."

Counting objects is easier than counting sounds as there is a visible representation for the children to look at and check their answer. With this method there is a way for them to check their answer afterwards.

This idea is a good example of linking skills across subjects, such as phonics and number. The Phase One phonics programme requires the children to listen carefully and discriminate sounds.

- Gather a selection of hard objects that will make a sound when dropped or thrown into a rigid container, such as a bucket.
- Hold the bucket so that the children cannot see what is inside it.
- Ask the children to close their eyes.
- Slowly drop the objects (for example marbles) into the bucket one at a time encouraging the children to count out loud to each sound they hear.
- When you have finished select a child to come out to the front and count the objects in the bucket – were they correct?
- Extend the idea by dropping the objects more quickly, or by asking the children to count silently in their heads.

Taking it further

If the children are good at counting, play the game backwards – tell them that there are ten marbles in the bucket to begin with and take some out to drop in another container. Ask the children how many marbles there are in each container. This requires the children to work with number bonds to ten and helps them to see the connection between addition and subtraction.

Response partners

"I like talking with my friend because she helps me to get my ideas straight in my head, and then when the teacher asks me I can let her share my ideas for me."

Using a response partner is an excellent way to get all the children in the group talking and sharing their ideas with one another. This increased participation means that low-level disruptive behaviour is reduced as the children are all engaged in the activity.

Including all the children in a starter session is a great way to move the lesson from good to outstanding. When working with response partners it requires participation from all the children. Depending upon the abilities of the children, you may wish to include the use of whiteboards, where one child can act as a scribe with the other's ideas.

- During a carpet teaching session, instead of asking one child to tell you about their holidays, for example, ask them all to turn to the person next to them and tell their response partner.
- Partners can be anyone who happens to be sitting next to each other, maybe someone different each day, or it could be a fixed partnership set by the teacher.
- For children who are reluctant to speak, ask the group, 'Who can tell me what their partner said? Tell me one of the words they used to describe the music.' This way reluctant children's ideas are shared without having to speak.
- If you have odd numbers simply ask the children to speak in a group of three.

Stars in their eyes

"I know that my child is really good at some things at home but I don't think that his school really knows about it. He is too little to go and tell his keyworker all about it and if I went in it would seem like showing off. I wish there were a better way."

Parental input into the child's developmental profile is crucial. By having a method of gathering data from parents and carers you can celebrate the child's achievements outside school.

- Cut out some star shapes from A4 coloured paper.
- Send one home to the parents and carers explaining that these are for them to write on when their child does something particularly well.
- They may choose things which are academic, sporty, kind, pastoral or out of the ordinary.
- The stars are brought back into the setting by the child and shared with the class before going on a display board for everyone to see.
- Have an envelope full of blank stars hanging near to the entrance door so that the parents and carers can take a few more whenever they please.

Teaching tip

If you find that you are collecting many stars from one particular family and none from another, change the way they are given out. Restrict them to a particular group of children, or if you want to find out something specific insist that stars are only for sport, music or extra-curricular activities.

Jigsaw experts

"I find this is a structured way to get all the children to take on a role, even the reluctant ones. As they are in a small group and clear with what they have to do they always complete the task."

A jigsaw group is one in which each member has a role, and fits together in a team like a jigsaw. The roles may include 'scribe', 'speaker' and 'observer' and each can be tailored to the developmental needs and abilities within the group.

- Decide on a task for the children to complete. It may be something practical like using the construction area to build a home for a soft toy, or looking outdoors in the natural environment for different kinds of leaves or seeds.
- Explain to the children that they will work in small groups of three or four, and that each person in the group has a specific role, but remind them frequently that it is very important to work together.
- Describe the roles to the children. For example, if the task is to gather natural materials, one child may need to decide where to look for such materials, another child to record by drawing the different leaves found and another to report the findings back to the class.
- Before beginning the task, ask the children to meet with similar members from the other groups to share ideas. So, for example, all the children who are deciding where to look will get together and discuss plans and ideas, as will the children who are to record and the children who are to report back. Then the children return to their original groups and begin the task.

Taking it further

This idea can be adapted to suit most topics and it can be used as a time-saving method by asking each group to research something different. For example, let the class look at a range of different objects from a history or religious topic and then feed back to the other children what they have found out.

Remember, remember

"As soon as I open the door in the morning many parents come to speak to me. I often forget which parent has said that their child is going home with someone else, or who would like a copy of a newsletter."

It can be difficult to remember the spoken messages from parents and carers at the beginning of each session, but it is obviously crucial to the children's well-being to do so. By jotting messages down you are able to transcribe them to a more relevant place when back in the classroom.

- Take a small notebook and pencil to the door when you greet parents.
- Use a different page – or double page spread – for each day.
- Write the day and date at the top of the page.
- Make quick notes when a parent or carer gives you a message.
- When you are back in the classroom, transfer the notes to a more appropriate place such as the whiteboard, register or going home timetable.
- Keep the notebook handy for other messages you may receive during the day.

Teaching tip

Hang the notebook on some string so that it can be kept on a hook near to the outside door. Do not be tempted just to use Post-it notes or a piece of scrap paper to record the messages – these are easily mislaid. You also may need to look back through the book at a later date, for example to see if a particular parent has collected other children before.

Medical needs

"My son is allergic to many things and has an EpiPen® containing adrenaline, to be used if he has a severe reaction. As there were so many staff in the Foundation setting I was very worried that that he could work with someone who didn't know what to do."

This is an extremely serious issue. There are usually many staff working in most Foundation Stage settings, and often these staff can change throughout the day and over lunchtime. By identifying the children at risk of a health issue with a photograph, all staff are aware of who to look out for and what to do should an emergency arise.

Teaching tip

Children often eat in a different part of the building and are supervised by different staff over lunchtime. Ensure that the poster is also displayed in the kitchen for the staff and that they know where the EpiPen® is kept and how to administer it.

- Obtain the parents or carers' permission to take a photograph of their child and display it in the setting.
- Explain to the parents or carers what the purpose of the poster is and clarify what information may go on it.
- Laminate the poster with the child's name and clear descriptions of the allergens or other medical needs.
- Use concise bullet points to act as a guide to first aid should a situation arise. For example, it may contain phrases such as, 'My name is Charlie Brown [include photo]. I am allergic to honey and nuts. If I touch or eat any of this I will have a severe and life-threatening allergic reaction. Please do the following:
  - Administer my EpiPen® immediately. It is kept in the kitchen on the left-hand shelf.
  - Telephone 999 and ask for an ambulance for anaphylactic shock.
  - Telephone my mum and tell her what has happened.
  - Keep me calm and warm, and comfort me until paramedics and/or my mum arrive.'

Going home timetable

"The children in our setting go to lots of different places after school, including after-school club, nursery, the school bus stop, to a sibling's classroom or to an extra-curricular activity in the hall such as ballet or football. Without the timetable I am sure I'd end up sending them to the wrong place!"

A large, clearly displayed timetable is invaluable to inform the practitioner which child is going where at the end of each day. It is also crucial should there be a supply practitioner who does not know the children and their daily routines.

- Make a large, blank, weekly timetable on A3 paper and laminate it.
- Write the days of the week along the side and different destinations across the top. These may include: nursery, after-school club, childminder, school bus, extra-curricular clubs such as ballet or football and grandparent's house.
- The only destination not to be labelled is going home with a parent or carer – assume this to be the norm.
- When you receive notification that a child is going to get the bus home every Thursday, for example, or collected by a childminder on Mondays and Tuesdays you can write the child's name in the appropriate space on the timetable.
- At home time go to the timetable and read out the named children first to line up in the appropriate place. The remaining children can then line up to be collected by their parent or carer.

Teaching tip

Throughout the session there are many occasions where you may think to yourself, 'I need to speak to that parent or carer about this at home time'. A brief look at the timetable will let you know whether this is possible that night or whether it will need to wait for another day, if a message should be written in the child's home school diary or whether it merits a telephone call.

Topical help

"Before we begin a new topic I always send a poster out to the parents and carers telling them what we are going to be doing. This is two-fold – as well as keeping them informed, it also supports my planning and provision through their contributions to the topic."

Parents and carers are an invaluable support to the curriculum. They are often able to supplement your provision with extra books and objects linked to the topic, so make sure you ask for their help!

Often at the beginning of the school year parents and carers complete an admission form and include information about their employment. This may be a valuable source of information giving a guide about possible support in school.

- Put together a simple A4 poster showing what will be covered over the next few weeks.
- Use pictures as well as text to make the poster accessible to all.
- Consider sending it out in alternative languages if it supports your catchment area.
- On the poster ask for any books or objects which may support the topic.
- Invite parents and carers with any experience in that field to come in and talk to the children about what they do.

Odd one out

"I love playing this game in the classroom. I'm really good at looking carefully and then choosing other children to stand in my group".

This game can fill five minutes at the beginning or end of a session. It requires the children to look carefully and make observations about the children standing in front of them.

The observational skills in this idea are transferable to many other activities, particularly science, art and mathematics.

- Choose two children to stand at the front of the group. Select them on the basis that they share a common criterion visible to the other children. This could be that they are both wearing a t-shirt the same colour, have a hair ribbon or are the same height.
- Ask the children to look carefully and think to themselves what they can see that is the same.
- Ask them to tell their response partner their observations.
- Select another child to come to the front and join the group, who also shares the same criterion.
- Ask the children to talk with their response partner – has this confirmed their answer as correct or incorrect?

Taking it further

If you think that you have children who are capable of choosing their own criteria, ask them to come out to the front and select children with similar aspects. If you want to extend the understanding of other children invite them to add children to the line-up. Check with the child who selected the original pair – does the line-up share a characteristic?

Dotty about the dot chart

"This is a really quick way to show that you are pleased with a child's behaviour and to reward them over time. It doesn't detract from the rest of the teaching and is a visible reminder to the children to behave well!"

A reward chart can sometimes be onerous to complete when you are 'in the moment' and teaching. The design of this chart lists the entire group and it is very easy to add points to for good behaviour.

Teaching tip

This also works for table groups. If the children regularly sit at the same table, identify the tables by name on a corner of the whiteboard. Each time the children on that table are well behaved award them a tally mark. Total up the tally at the end of the week and reward them with a sticker or a small reward, such as extra playtime or choice of computer activity.

This idea works well when the children regularly sit in the same place in front of the adult. A quick glance at the chart works wonders with children trying to achieve more points!

- Write a list of children's names on the left hand side of a piece(s) of A4 or A3 lined paper.
- Laminate the paper.
- Attach it to the wall next to where you usually sit to talk to the children.
- Have a whiteboard pen nearby or on a piece of string attached to the wall.
- Explain to the children that when they behave well or achieve something they have been working towards you will put a small dot next to their name with the felt pen.
- Add dots each time the children reach their achievements or demonstrate good behaviour.
- The dots can be counted up and praise/ reward given either after a set period of time, say a week, or when the children have reached a certain number of dots, for example ten.

Standing straight!

"I worked with a four-year-old girl who struggled with the expectations of behaviour in the class. Lining-up time and sitting on the floor were two particular challenges for her. The photographs really made it easy for her to see what was required, and her behaviour improved."

Young children in a new setting can find it difficult to understand what is expected of them at first, and may need a more detailed explanation. By re-enacting lining up or sitting on the carpet for them to look at and analyse, they are able to see how to achieve what the teacher asks.

- Select a small group of around six children to stand in a line, as though waiting for lunch or to leave a room.
- Walk up and down the line with the child who finds it difficult, looking and commenting upon how the children are standing.
- Identify the following: which way are the children facing? Which way are their shoes pointing?
- Make a physical space in the middle of the line for your child to stand in. Help them to slot into the line and make sure they are facing the right way and that their feet are oriented the correct way.
- Take a photograph of the line.
- Afterwards, print out the photograph and talk with the child (or children) about what makes it a smart line; is anyone talking? Are they standing behind each other?
- Repeat the physical standing line with larger groups of children and with less intervention from an adult until the child can join the line independently.

Teaching tip

Photographs such as these make an effective display. Talk with the children about what makes a harmonious setting (orderliness, friendliness, politeness, listening, turn-taking etc.). Use the photographs as talking points in carpet discussions. Equip the children with a camera and encourage them to use it to take photographs of each other behaving in a desirable manner. Print these out and let the children talk about them during PHE.

My button family

"This little button game has revolutionised the way I gather information from the children about who is in their family, where they live and about any other significant relationships they may have".

As a practitioner, it is crucial to know about the family members the child has, and their relationships and feelings towards them. Young children can find it difficult to verbalise their thoughts and feelings, and this little game opens up a discussion without the need for eye contact or intense question and answer sessions.

Before beginning the following idea it is very important to know if any individual children have problems at home or have complex family backgrounds.

- Gather together a collection of buttons in a box. Include different sizes, colours and designs.
- Sit beside the child, as the lack of eye-contact can make it easier for children to communicate.
- Tip out the button box and let the child look through them and handle them.
- Explain that you would like them to choose a button that represents them the most and to put it on the table. The size, style and position of the button on the table may give you an indication of how the child sees themselves. For example, it may be a bright colour and large size, suggesting confidence, placed in the centre of the table.
- Ask the child to think about other people who are important to them, such as family members.
- Tell the child that you would like them to look through the buttons and choose one to represent another person, and to put it on the table.

- The colour, size and shape of this button may reflect the child's emotions towards the person. It may also be significant which family member they choose first. For example, on a very simplistic level it may be that they choose an attractive button in a bright colour and put it next to their button to represent their primary carer, or a large button in a dark foreboding colour to represent an absent parent or carer. Where they position these buttons in relation to their own is also significant.
- Afterwards glue the buttons to a piece of paper and label them as a record of the conversation, or take a digital photograph and annotate it.

If this exercise is done at the beginning of the school year it allows the practitioner to understand the home situations of their pupils. This enables understanding around separated parents who may require additional copies of letters or separate appointments on parents' evening, or the difficulties faced by children whose parents have an acrimonious relationship and the complexities of leaving school shoes or reading books at one home for a week until the next visit.

Character 'king of the castle'

"I struggled to explore character with my reception class. By using the puppets it became easy for them to see how the characters developed throughout the story."

For this activity, choose puppets that represent the two main characters in the story, preferably a 'goody' and a 'baddy'. By moving them up and down a vertical hill, or wall, the children are able to begin to explore the emotions of the character or their moral position in the story.

Character puppets can be expensive. A simple laminated picture on a lollipop stick is enough to stimulate the children's imaginations.

- Create a physical 'castle' – use a box or table with a drape over it.
- Begin telling a familiar fairy tale to the children. Stop when the main character is at a key point in the story.
- Using the character puppet or toy, put it in an appropriate position. For example, in the story of 'The Three Little Pigs', the wolf is at the top of the 'hill' and the pigs are at the bottom when the wolf is trying and succeeding in blowing down the first two houses. However, when the wolf fails to destroy the third house the roles are reversed and the pigs become successful.
- Talk with the children about how the roles and positions change as the story moves on.
- Used skilfully, this approach can help children to understand their own behaviour and appropriate responses to unwanted bad behaviour of others. For instance, reporting hurtful behaviour to an adult leaves the innocent child on 'high ground'. Retaliating and hurting the child who hurt them initially results in both children being at the 'bottom of the hill'.

Taking it further

This activity works well outside where there are lots of places to put a character. Let the children decide where to put it – for example the top of the climbing frame, in the sand pit. Let them run around to find a good place, and then go together to find it. Discuss who chose the place, why they chose it and which part of the story it represents.

Let's go fishing

"I find that when the children are playing in the water, particularly with fishing nets, they seem to forget they are learning! I have found that most areas of the curriculum can be 'fished for', and I love the fact that this activity is really successful outside."

You can use fishing nets to identify, group or order specific items or objects with similar characteristics. These can be simple either/or definitions (float or sink) or more complex (ordering heaviest to lightest).

Decide upon the topic to be investigated and the learning objective. This can be linked to the topic or be a standalone objective. Prompt the children to use appropriate vocabulary relevant to the objective.

- Obtain a variety of fishing nets to use in the water tray. Include nets of different shape and size such as seaside rock pool nets, butterfly nets, sieves, tea leaf strainers and washing powder tablet net bags. Cut any long handles down if necessary.
- Put some appropriate items in the tray and explain the activity to the children. Ideas may include gathering and sorting between upper and lower case letters; ordering alphabetically; ordering numerals; 'fishing' for animals which live in different environments; sorting objects of different colour/material/weight/shape; collecting items that roll/are used for eating food/are natural/artificial.
- Let them explore and investigate the items and display their findings.
- There are many possibilities suited to almost every topic or theme.

Teaching tip

To record the outcome of the children's investigation in an activity such as this it is useful to ask them to display their findings. This can be as simple as laying out the objects in two groups (for example floats/sinks; even/odd) or in a line ordered from one outcome to another (for example numbers 1-10; alphabetical order; heaviest to lightest; oldest to youngest). To capture the transiency of this result use a digital camera to take a quick photo before putting the objects back into the water tray for the next group of children.

Size doesn't matter – shape does!

"The psychologist Jean Piaget investigated how young children comprehend conservation of number. I did this task as part of a topic on size and shape, but it would fit into any mathematics topic, and is great to investigate outdoors."

Bottles and containers come in all shapes and sizes. It can be difficult for children to appreciate that the size and shape of the container can vary widely whilst the volume remains the same.

Piaget's theory of conservation stated that children aged between four and seven years old are initially unaware that altering a substance's appearance does not change its basic properties.

Piaget's most famous experimental task involved a child being presented with two identical beakers containing the same amount of liquid. The child usually notes that the beakers do contain the same amount of liquid. When one of the beakers is poured into a taller and thinner container, children who are younger than seven or eight years old typically say that the two beakers no longer contain the same amount of liquid, and that the taller container holds the larger quantity, without taking into consideration the fact that both beakers were previously noted to contain the same amount of liquid. Due to superficial changes, the child was unable to comprehend that the properties of the substances continued to remain the same (conservation).

This idea explores this developmental stage in more detail.

- Ask the children to bring in empty bottles and containers, preferably with labels with the volume listed in millilitres. Include tiny bottles such as food colouring bottles, familiar shampoo bottles and large bottles such as milk containers.
- Fill the bottles with coloured water to emphasise that they hold liquid.
- Talk about the difference in appearance of the bottles. Let the children look at them, handle them and pass them around before putting them back in the middle of the circle.
- Through discussion, encourage the children to put the bottles on the carpet in a line of which holds most to least volume.
- Talk about how volume is measured – let the children to look at the labels on the bottles and find the volume of each.
- Draw these on a flip chart inside a rough outline of each bottle shape.
- Ask the children to make the line in order of volume again – is it different this time? How? Talk about the findings together.

Taking it further

Fill the containers with lentils, sand or tea leaves and put them into the water or dry tray. Let the children investigate filling and pouring before ordering them by volume. Take a photograph of their findings and put on a labelled display, so they can compare their line with that of their friends.

Bingo!

"I love playing bingo! We play it in all different lessons on our whiteboards – and the winner gets a sticker!"

Bingo is a great plenary activity and can be used in many subjects to varying degrees of complexity. Children start by picking a small selection of the correct possible answers to put in their grid, making the game a listening and following instructions task.

Tell the children that to play bingo they must first write a different answer in each of the sections they have drawn on their whiteboard and that they should cross it out when the teacher calls out that answer.

- Show the children how to draw a horizontal mid-line on their individual whiteboard, and to add one or two vertical lines depending on the size of grid required.
- Depending upon the topic, you may have generated a list of possible answers on the board for the children to pick from. To add challenge you can ask them to write 'words with the "ee" phoneme', or 'even numbers under 10'. Say the answers, giving the children time to cross out any answers they have on their whiteboards.
- It is important that the children only draw a line through their answer and not cross it out entirely, as their answers will be unverifiable and they will not get a sticker!
- Decide whether the children need to cross out a line of answers or get a 'full house' before they can call bingo! (or a topic-linked word, for example 'Insect!' if you are studying mini-beasts.)
- Award the winner a sticker after checking their answers.

Guess who!

"This game requires the children to listen and respond to a variety of adjectives. I use it to enrich different topics, and I use it as a tool for Assessment for Learning, too!"

By standing up or sitting down with a photo card when the teacher describes a specific characteristic of a creature or object, the children can work together to find out its identity – a sort of collaborative, 3D 'Guess Who!'

- Give each child a card with a photo on it. This may be linked to characters in traditional tales, items linked to a topic studied, for example vehicles or creatures, or phonemes from your literacy planning.
- Explain to the children that you have chosen one of their photos as the 'winner', but that you are not going to tell them immediately which that is. They are going to listen carefully to the descriptions you are giving and work out if theirs is the winner.
- Ask all the children to stand up.
- Say something simple to begin with, such as, 'The winner is a female character', or 'The winner has wings/more than two wheels'.
- Explain to the children that they must sit down if the picture on their card means they cannot be the winner.
- The first time you play, it may be useful to have an additional adult walking around the group and checking who is sitting down, as children can be confused that they must sit down if they *don't* have the photo with wings/wheels.

Teaching tip

At first, play this game in pairs or threes. This way the children can share ideas and listen together, gaining confidence and learning from each other. Remember to match your descriptive terms to the understanding and language capabilities of the children.

Make a shape!

"We play this game in P.E. all the time. We help the teacher to choose three animals for us to pretend to be, and then we make the shapes when the music stops. I don't like being out, but we play it a lot so sometimes I win!"

This idea helps the children to improve their listening and to follow instructions, particularly when under a time constraint.

Teaching tip

Many children will change their animal shape to another one after you have uncovered your eyes – to avoid being 'out'. Cover and uncover your eyes very elaborately so they can see you looking the moment you say the name. It will help if you peep through the cracks in your fingers, or recruit another adult or the other children as spies for cheats!

This game requires space to play, so move the furniture or use a large space like the hall.

- Choose three animals that the children can imitate. It is best to select three animals that look completely different to each other, in order to reduce confusion when identifying which one the children are imitating are. For example, a giraffe, elephant and snake are better than a cat, dog and horse.
- Show the children how to use their whole body to make the shape of each animal.
- Play some music, or shake a tambourine and allow the children to move around the space and pretend to be any animal they like.
- Cover your eyes and stop the music.
- Remind the children that they have to make the shape of a giraffe, elephant or snake immediately, and freeze!
- Without looking, say the name of one of the animals.
- Open your eyes and ask all the children who chose to imitate the named animal that they are 'out' and must sit at the side.
- Remind the children that they have to pretend to be a different animal each time. Repeat until almost all the children are out and you have one or two 'winning' children remaining.

The first one to fetch...

"This is a great ten minute activity to suit all situations – on an educational visit, in the park, on holiday or even on the beach! It requires the children to listen carefully, look around, run about and observe their environment."

By sending the children out into the immediate environment to collect an object and return to you with it, they are exercising not only their bodies but also their ears and eyes! This game can also include a competitive element as the 'first one back' or 'first to touch' (for example a tree).

Before beginning this game it is worth spending a few minutes practising gathering together, running away and then coming back when the whistle blows. Give out some stickers to the winners to encourage a speedy return!

- Gather the children around you.
- Explain that they are going to listen carefully to the request and then run off to find whatever you ask for.
- In some cases they are able to bring it back, for example 'something green', 'something with lines on it', 'something with letters on it'.
- Tailor your request to the environment you are in and thus the topic you are working on.
- If the children are able to follow more complex instructions let them work in pairs with two-step instructions or to collect two objects, for example 'something that has grown, and has been green; something that has never been alive and something that has'. Vary these requests according to the knowledge of the children and the themes they have covered in science – you may need to give an example.

Taking it further

Let the children bring a digital camera to collect images when you are all out and about. Give them a list of items to collect an image of – five green things; three round things, two smooth things and something that rolls. This enables them to 'collect' (by photograph) items which are too big to carry for example drainpipes, statues and trees!

Outdoor motoring maths

"Numbers outdoors are really useful, especially when linked to the outdoor play area. Boys particularly love the topic of vehicles and journeys, so this is ideal for introducing numerals and the number system in a natural and purposeful manner."

By being creative with how numbers are placed around the outdoor learning environment helps children to use them naturally and gradually become more familiar with them.

To prompt the children to look around their environment for numbers, create a display with photographs of numbers in the environment. Encourage the children to take their own photographs or make drawings of numbers in their homes and add these to the display.

- Consider how numbers could be used in your outdoor environment. There will probably be bikes, cars or areas outdoors where labels and numerals can replicate the use of numbers in everyday life.

- Laminate some large numbers to attach to the wheeled toys (bikes, tricycles, scooters etc.) so that the children can 'park' them in numerical order at the end of the day.

- Create large, numbered 'parking bays' using chalk or laminated signs so that the children can put the wheeled toys away in the appropriate (matching) numbered bay.

- Have a large clock outside so that they can look at the time and the numerals on the clock face.

- Make 'bus stops' so that the children can practise being bus drivers and 'drive' to each stop in numerical order. Move these around frequently so they take a different route each day.

Taking it further

Create a real 'bus driver' game where the children visit each stop in turn, with a container. Have a dice and a box of small counting objects (play people are ideal) at each stop. When they stop, they roll the dice and 'pick up' the matching number of objects (or passengers) from the box of objects. When they arrive back at the 'bus depot' the winner is the driver with the most 'passengers'. This game can also be played using the entire class as life-sized passengers!

Listening, turning, pointing...'Over there!'

"Sometimes when we go outside we play this game for a few minutes, and I always like it because it's really easy! I like closing my eyes and spinning and you don't need to look at the board or do any reading or anything so it's really good!"

Some children struggle to achieve academically in the learning environment, and it is refreshing to find an activity in which all the children have a similar chance of achieving. This idea works anywhere there are background noises, indoors or outdoors.

Before beginning this idea check that none of the children have hearing problems. Some may hear better on one side than the other, so look carefully at their position and ensure they are standing in the appropriate place.

- Stand the children in front of you, with enough space around them so they can each turn around with outstretched arms.
- Ask them to close their eyes.
- Explain that they are going to listen carefully for a noise. When they hear it they are to turn around to face the direction of the sound, and wait for the command to open their eyes. The sound they hear may be traffic outside, the noise from another room or a door opening.
- When everyone has their eyes open, select a child who has turned and ask everyone to turn to face the same direction.
- Ask the child to tell the rest of the class what they can hear.
- Listen carefully together, and if the other children hear the same sound ask them to point to where it came from.
- Repeat, listening carefully for other sounds.

Teaching tip

If you cannot find a place with background sounds create your own! Use familiar sounds (a spoon in a cup, mobile phone ringtones, ice cubes in a glass, a hairdryer) and move around the children to create the sounds in different areas of the setting.

Stand on something...blue!

"This is a great outdoors game. I like playing it best with a partner, because we are both really fast at finding the colours to stand on!"

This game is reliant upon there being a coloured, painted surface on the ground. For example, markings for a tennis or football pitch, a coloured play surface or markings for playground games such as hopscotch and snakes and ladders.

If there are no existing markings you could play a simple version of this idea outdoors on a day when the ground is half wet and half dry, and appears to be different colours.

- Gather the children together outdoors.
- Draw their attention to the markings on the ground. Talk about the colours and shapes that they can see.
- Ensure that all the children know the meaning of the words curved, straight etc., and the names of the colours and shapes.
- Tell the children that you are going to ask them to run to a particular colour or shape and they have to find it and stand on it as quickly as they can.
- Say the following: 'Everyone stand on something...blue!'
- Watch the children scramble to find a blue line, shape or image to stand on.
- Repeat the request with things that are different colours or shapes, for example 'Stand on a curved line!' 'Stand on a red square!'

Taking it further

The children can play this game in pairs; you still ask them to find a particular colour or shape but the children must find a piece of marking big enough to stand on whilst holding hands with their partner. To further extend this, ask them to go to two colours, so the pair can stand on one each.

100 square outdoor bingo

"I initially taught my children this game as part of an outdoor maths lesson, using beanbags. I was delighted when I saw them playing it at playtime, self-initiating a game using stones they had found in the garden!"

If there is only one painting on the ground in the outdoor area, a 100 square is hard to beat for value for money. There are many different games to play on it – the kinetic and competitive aspects of this one make it appealing to most children.

It may be possible to chalk a number square on the ground if there are no permanent markings already.

- You will need two large foam dice and some beanbags or large counters to cover the numbers on the ground.
- Show the children how to roll both dice and put the numbers side by side to create a two-digit number. Ensure that the children understand that this is not addition, they only need to create a two-digit number.
- Ask them to put their beanbag on the square that shows the number rolled.
- Repeat rolling the dice and creating numbers. The winner is the first child to put three beanbags in a row, either horizontally or vertically.
- There are many variations on this – the first child to cover three numbers with the number '5' in it, or a whole column of '2s'.
- Match the complexity of the game to the ability of the children playing.
- Use chalk to create a simpler number grid if your children are working on smaller numbers, or if you wish to add the dice totals and look at number bonds, for example.

Taking it further

Have a set of smaller 100 squares and a box of interesting counters (varied buttons or dried beans and pulses) in your setting because the children will often play with them independently and make up their own variations of the original game. It does not matter what they actually do – as long as they are saying the number names and looking at the pattern of the numerals they will become more familiar with the idea of counting and the number system.

Outdoor orienteering

"Children love running around outside. This idea is like a treasure hunt, and includes clues and objects to collect as rewards!"

Use the outdoor area to introduce children to numbers, letters or objects linked to a theme. Children follow picture clues around the setting in order to collect laminated pictures or different coloured objects.

This idea works well if the children have a prop or piece of clothing to really get in the mood for finding treasure! This may be a pirate hat or a pair of binoculars or anything else from the dressing up box. If they work in pairs or teams they could have the same colour band as the rest of their team.

- Select an area for the children to explore. Ensure that there are some places to hide a laminated postcard or a small box with objects, such as a box of shells, a box of pinecones, a box of gravel, a box of leaves or a box of twigs.
- If you wish you can use small items from the setting which are different colours, such as red bricks, yellow bricks, green bricks etc.
- Explain to the children that they are going to go outside and search for picture clues.
- Give them a small sandwich bag or a basket to collect their cards or objects in.
- Begin by giving them a picture card with a drawing of a place on. For example, this may be the climbing frame, playhouse, sand tray or a tree.
- Explain to the children that they are to run to the object pictured and look for two things – an object to put in their bag and another picture clue (which will lead them to another place to find treasure).

- Help them to identify the next object to run to.
- When they have run out of clues ask them to return to you and share their 'spoils' – check they have collected the correct number or range of colours of items.

Bonus idea

Instead of giving the children a bag to collect physical objects, supply paper on a clipboard to enable them to record by drawing or writing the object, letter or numeral they find at each 'hiding' place.

To introduce ICT into the idea, equip each child with a digital camera so that they can take a photograph of each object or word at each place.

To make this into a music or listening idea put an instrument or recording of a sound at each place. If the children are familiar with using them, simple sound tins or flip cameras work well for this. Equip the children with a means of recording the sound of each instrument in order, or with a clipboard to record through drawing and emergent writing what sound they can hear on the recording at each point. For example, birds, mobile phone ring tones, doorbell, ice cream van music, etc.

To make this idea resemble actual orienteering as much as possible, hang a hole punch on a string at each point. It is possible to buy single hole punches that punch different shapes. By supplying the children with an 'orienteering' card (for example a used birthday card) they are able to punch differently shaped holes as they identify each point through pictures.

Taking it further

To extend the idea further or link to a current topic hide letters, numerals and key words for the children to copy onto their card at several places around the setting. When they return, arrange the letters or numbers in order to spell a word or sequence numbers in a pattern or help them to sort items in terms of size or by colour if more appropriate to the children's level.

Posting postcards

"Children love to get things in the post. It seems to be a miracle when the postcard they created away from home actually drops through their letterbox!"

Blank postcards can be used to teach the children about how the postal system works and also helps them to learn their address.

Ensure you have the correct address for each child in the group. You may need to confirm this with their parents/carers before the teaching session.

- Provide each child with a blank sticker to take home for their parents to write their address on. If you do not have stickers send home the blank white postcard for the parents to address directly.
- Tell the parents/carers that this is going to be sent through the post and they must leave one side completely blank so that the children can draw a picture on it.
- Show some examples of picture postcards to the children. This works best if the pictures are of places that are known or relevant to the children in that particular setting.
- Let the children draw on their postcard, write their name on the back and affix a stamp.
- Walk together to the nearest post box and let each child put their card in the box, explaining that the postman will collect their postcards from the box and that they will arrive at their homes in the next few days.
- Make a display space for the children to bring in their cards the following week.

Taking it further

Use this as a transition activity by asking children to send a postcard during the holidays. Give them the details of their new setting, class or keyworker on a sticker for them to fix to a holiday postcard or Christmas/Happy New Year card (depending upon their culture and religion). These can be put up as a display and shared with the new teacher and class after the break.

The moving bus

"When I had to move into Year One I was really worried about where to go and what the teacher would be like, but after the visit I felt loads better as I knew what to expect."

By spending a little time on transition between classes or key stages in a school the children are comforted and informed about what their next class will be like and where it is. As part of this, a display with photographs of their new class will begin to create a team or group identity.

There may be some children for whom it is not possible to display a named photograph, due to safeguarding concerns. If this is the case ensure that the display uses the same protocol for all the children so there is not an obvious 'odd one out'.

- Arrange for the children to spend a little time in their new class with their new teacher or keyworker.
- Play some games to help the children get to know each other and begin to foster a team identity.
- Take a head and shoulders photograph of each child.
- Create a large 2D picture of a bus and display it on the wall.
- Add the children's individual photographs and display as though they are looking through the windows of the bus.
- Include each child's name directly under their photograph.
- Ensure the display is somewhere immediately visible and at a level where the children can see each other's' photographs.
- Alter the type of vehicle if you need extra (a train) or less (a car) spaces.

Teaching tip

Make this part of an entire transport display, using different types of vehicle for differently sized groups of children. Add to it when the children are in your group by inviting them to bring in photos from home of them travelling on different types of vehicle – from their bikes and scooters outdoors or even riding a donkey on the beach!

The free workforce!

"As one of only two adults in a busy Foundation setting, my time is extremely precious. I used to spend ages washing and cleaning the toys, until it occurred to me that the children would love this job, and with only a few tweaks it actually became educational."

There are many items in a Foundation unit which need regular cleaning. By putting them in the water tray with some safe bubbles or detergent, such as baby bubble bath, the children are able to play with them and sort them without realising they are actually cleaning them too!

Almost all children love playing in water, particularly with bubbles. Ensure you have aprons ready to keep their clothes dry.

- Find a space suitable for the children to use water and bubbles. It is best to do this outdoors.
- Fill the water tray or a similar large container, such as a small inflatable paddling pool with water. Make bubbles with baby bubble bath or use a similar safe detergent.
- Put a plastic box of items you wish to be cleaned and sorted at the side, and place a towel on the floor.
- Let the children tip the objects into the water and show them how to clean them. Add cloths and different brushes to let them scrub!
- Explain to the children that they have to put the cleaned objects on the towel. Let them sort or group the items by size, colour or nature by putting out different coloured towels for the objects to dry on.

Taking it further

Create a role-play situation that involves cleaning the toys. For example, when outdoors the cars, bikes and scooters can be involved in a car wash; indoors, the dolls and babies can be part of a baby clinic complete with bath.

Personal effects

"Beginning pre-school at two and a half years old can be quite intimidating – for many children this is their first independent time away from home. This idea helps them to bring a little of themselves to the setting and easily identify their peg and their tray drawer."

Most children have one or two pre-visits to a setting before they begin attending more regularly. This is an opportunity to explain to their parents and carers that some small stickers, pictures of objects or characters to stick on their pegs will help with identification and will be familiar, comforting symbols for the children in the setting.

To make identification even easier, use similar colour themes on both pegs and tray labels to help the children to find their belongings.

- Have some pre-cut outlines of card shapes.
- Write the first name of each child on the shape before their visit, and lay the shapes out on a table. It is useful to use different colours or shapes (bears, cars, cats, kites etc.) to aid identification.
- On each child's first visit, take them to these shapes and help them to find their name. Together, take the shape to the pegs and let the child choose a peg, or guide them to the one you have chosen for them.
- Attach the shape label to the peg, and help the child to hang up their belongings.
- Explain that this is their peg each time they visit, and that they are welcome to bring in some stickers or pictures from home to decorate their label.
- Look together at the labels of other children – are there any recognisable characters?

Teaching tip

This idea also gives you an opening conversation to have with shy or quiet children. If the child is clearly a big fan of a particular book, provide it in the reading corner and encourage them to read it or quietly share the book together. The child will be comforted by this familiarity and will enjoy telling you what they know about the characters.

Get ready for summer!

"Summer always drives me crazy – sunhats, water bottles and sun creams for every child simply take over the setting! A hat box and sun cream basket help to simplify getting ready for time outdoors."

It is important that young children learn how to organise themselves and become more independent, but this can take a lot of time out of the day. By limiting their choices and providing well-ordered storage-children are able to find and use their belongings appropriately.

Look carefully at the environment in the setting to make sure that it enables the children to be independent. Remember to crouch down and be the same height as the children – is everything still accessible and clearly visible?

- Ensure that all hats, water bottles and sun creams are labelled.
- Have a hat box large enough to hold all the sun hats and keep it near to the entrance. Establish the routine of coming in and taking hats off to put in the box, and leaving the room and putting hats on. This enables you to quickly look in the box and identify who has forgotten their sun hat.
- Water bottles – if they are stored at the side of the room children often forget they are there! Put a little basket on the table they sit at so their drink is in front of them all the time. If they do not have fixed places, provide several baskets in different areas of the setting so they can easily find their own. Colour code the baskets if necessary.
- Sun cream can also be stored in baskets of small groups so that the children can find their own independently and where appropriate, apply it under the supervision of an adult.

What's on the whiteboard today?

"As a parent I never know what the children have been doing during the day. I look at the whiteboard in the window every morning – it gives me something to ask them about on the way home!"

A whiteboard hanging in the window where the parents and carers gather makes it possible for the adults dropping off or collecting to look at what is happening today, tomorrow, or what has happened that day. This enables them to bring the correct equipment for their child and ask them specific questions about their day.

- Obtain a large whiteboard, about the size of an A1 poster. If you cannot find a whiteboard it is possible to buy adhesive vinyl in plain colours to stick over a pin board or similar.
- Divide the board into two sections – the upper two thirds to be labelled 'today' and the smaller bottom section to be labelled 'tomorrow'.
- Write two or three bullet points under each heading to inform the parents and carers. For example, you could write:

Today:
- We will be looking at 3D shapes and making buildings
- We are practising the songs for our show.

Tomorrow:
- We will be doing P.E. in the hall – remember your P.E. kit!

Teaching tip

The board can also be used for on-going reminders if you want the parents and carers to remember things or bring items in, for example add a bubble on the bottom requesting boxes for box modelling, spare clothes for the emergency box or books related to a forthcoming topic. Remember to also use the board to thank the parents and carers for their help.

101

Observing in order

"The EYFS asks us to look at the children's attitudes to learning as well as their achievements. By planning this into one or two activities each week and working on a strict rota we found it much easier to collect evidence and had lots of knowledge by the time we completed the profile in June."

Observation needs to be part of the routine in any early years setting, but it can easily be forgotten over the course of a busy session. Sometimes the only observations noted are the 'incredible moments' or those moments where a child makes a surprising or unexpected development – this idea will help you to observe the child frequently and regularly.

Ensure that all the staff in the setting understand how the following idea works.

- Have a box of index cards with a child's name on each one.
- Keep these in an elastic band or small box to preserve their order.
- Plan in a time every few sessions for observation. Ensure that there are enough members of staff to enable the observation to take place uninterrupted.
- Take a card from the box and decide whether you wish to observe the child doing a specific activity or whether you want them to self-select areas within the setting.
- Observe the child for a short time, noting down what they are saying, doing, and playing.
- Note on the index card the time, date, duration and purpose of the observation.
- Return the index card to the back of the box and look at the next card to identify the next child for observation.

Taking it further

To identify children's different learning styles or attitudes to learning observe a small group undertaking a planned problem-solving activity where they can work as a team or individually to solve a query, for example filling water containers in the water tray or building a tower or bridge using a limited number of objects to 'rescue' a character.

Planning for everyone

"The key things with plans are that they are useful and used. Different plans have different purposes but by displaying them on the wall everyone will know what to set up, in which area and the learning objective for each activity."

Plans should be amended, scribbled on and visible for all of the team. A central display board with all the planning in addition to specific boards in each room or area ensures that all staff are always aware of what is required in the setting.

There are such a variety of plans that it is nearly impossible to create a definitive version for all settings to use. However, some plans are routinely used – timetables of staff responsibilities, organisational plans showing which activities are set up on which table and when adults are to supervise each area.

If each member of staff has a different planning responsibility it helps to increase the importance of the planning. Even the responsibility of setting up the learning environment following the planning raises the profile of the planning wall in this idea.

- Choose a large wall with space for different plans and rotas on A3 and A4 paper.
- Ensure it is in a place where staff will walk past and be able to study it.
- Decide which plans you need to display and position them roughly on the wall.
- Put display paper on the wall and mount card behind each plan.
- Staple a plastic wallet on top of each mounting. This way photocopied plans can simply be slipped into each wallet and neatly display mounted.
- Encourage staff to add comments and look at the board frequently.
- Change the relevant plans each week.

Teaching tip

After the activity don't throw the plan away, but file it with comments added as to how this could work better next time. This makes it much easier to plan a similar topic again and also to reflect with colleagues about what worked well in that topic.

Involving parents/carers

"My favourite thing is showing my daddy what I've done. He is usually at work so when it's 'Daddy Day' I'm so pleased to show everyone my dad!"

Some parents can be hard to reach, but by putting on an event just before pick up time the children will pester their parents and carers into attending. If the beginning of the day works better, open the doors early and provide tea and coffee.

Teaching tip

Make a display with photographs of the children with their relative. This will act as a talking point for the children to discuss with other adults and children in the setting.

Before going ahead with a session designed specifically for a particular parent (for example Daddy Day, Grandparents' Day) ensure that each of the children will have someone to invite, for example Grandparent's Day could include aunties and uncles.

If the setting is part of a larger establishment such as the Foundation Stage of a larger school, consider inviting the other year groups.

- Be clear about the focus of the session and what you need to achieve to enable the session to be a success, for example if you want to promote boys' reading, invite male relatives to bring along their favourite books.
- Think about your class and whether they will all have someone to invite.
- Let the parents and carers know of the date of the event in plenty of time, to allow them to arrange childcare or book time off work.
- Include the children in the planning: making posters, invitations, lists of snacks needed or in re-arranging the environment.
- Warmly welcome the adults into the setting, allowing the children time to greet their relatives and show them around.
- You could ask the adults to work with the children to draw pictures of what activities they liked to do when they were small, or to read books and comics together.

Morning challenges

"I can't wait to see what the morning challenge is when I get to school. It's always something fun and easy to do."

When the children come in each morning it helps them to settle and be calm if they have a routine to follow or a task to complete. This idea also enables the children to practise and consolidate skills learnt earlier in the week.

Choose five ideas linked to the topics and themes covered that week. They might be linked to maths, art, literacy or science, and they could involve using pencil and paper, designing and making or construction.

Teaching tip

Set up the tasks at the end of each day ready for the next morning. If you have a child who is a good reader they could help you to set up at the end of each day.

- This idea works in a carousel manner, where five activities are rotated around the groups each morning so that each child has done all activities by the end of the week.
- Select five activities which the children can attempt independently. Some ideas include: building something linked to the theme with construction; cutting and sticking items from a catalogue; drawing pictures or maps; sorting and grouping coloured objects, shapes or numbers; reading books around a topic; finding information from a webpage or collecting data from each other and recording it however they choose.
- Briefly explain each activity to the children before the first session begins.
- Put the items required for each activity on each table or area. Display a sign or notice at each of these areas so the children know which activity to go to when they arrive.
- Encourage the children to work independently at their task. The adult may decide to take the register whilst the class are engaged.

105

Journey sticks

"Going on walks or adventures with young children is great, but on their return to the classroom they have often forgotten where they have been and what they have seen! When my class made a journey stick it helped them to remember their adventures."

On a walk or visit in the environment this idea helps the children to record what they see or encounter along the way. With care these can be put in order to extend their understanding of sequencing and ordinal language.

This idea requires a little preparation, using either lollipop sticks or twigs with a long piece of wool or string attached to the top.

- Before the walk, give each child a pre-prepared journey stick.
- Explain that as they walk through their environment they are to collect items which will remind them of what they can see.
- With help, they are to attach an item from each part of the walk onto their journey stick, recording their journey. For example, they may walk along a gravelly path where they could tie a stone on to the string on the stick; through a field – tie on some grass; past a duck pond – tie on a feather; through a garden – tie on some petals.
- On return to the setting use the journey sticks as prompts to talk about the experience.
- Display the sticks alongside photographs of the key points on the journey. Be ready for the children to collect items which you were not prepared for – litter and sweet wrappings are always popular!

Bonus idea ★

Use these journey sticks as a prompt to write about or talk about the journey, using structured support such as a writing frame with sections headed 'first, second, then, next, finally'. Model saying and writing a simple sentence using key words, for example 'First I saw a tree. Next I saw a pond. Then I saw a path.' This task can be made as simple or complicated as necessary.

Sticky colour strips

"Colour is a really inclusive teaching tool. Most children can see and distinguish between colours and this activity ensures all children can achieve attractive results."

This idea looks at colour, shade and tone in the natural environment. Initially, children acknowledge colours simply — green, red, blue, yellow. By introducing them to the idea that there are many different shades of particular colours and that some of these have different names (for example, green can also be lime, turquoise etc.), children begin to see the world around them with more precision.

Colour charts from DIY stores are an excellent visual demonstration that there are many different shades of each colour. Collect a few of these together to use outdoors when looking at the environment.

- Use a strip of thick card with double-sided carpet tape attached along the length.
- Peel off the top sticky side to create a sticky strip of card.
- Let the children explore a natural environment, for example, collecting items in shades of green; blades of grass and leaves.
- Stick these onto the sticky strip to create a colour chart.
- Encourage them to work from light to dark shades along their stick.
- By sticking the double-sided tape onto the colour strip from the DIY store the children can search and match objects and items in the actual shades of green on the chart.

Taking it further

Have a bag of pieces of coloured wool. At frequent points throughout the walk gather the children together and look around at what they can see. Let them look through the wool bag and choose a piece which colour or texture represents what they can see — red for house roofs, brown for fences, yellow for hay in the fields. Wrap these carefully around the sticky card strip. Use this as an aide memoire on return to the setting.

My tree

"I love working outdoors. It doesn't really feel like work, but I still do lots of drawing, writing and finding out with my friends."

This idea works well at a park or area with a variety of trees. The children can work in small adult-led groups to find out lots about one important aspect of the natural environment — the trees.

Adult guidance is important to get the children to focus in detail on their tree. Try to get enough adult helpers to allow small groups of about four or five children per adult.

- Explain to the children that they are going to work together to find out all they can about one tree.
- Let the groups choose their own tree from the environment.
- Make little packs for the adult to take outside. Include simple folded books, tape measures, a camera, pencils, crayons, wax crayons, sticky tape and glue.
- Give each child in the group a simple folded book and ask them to write their name on the front.
- Collect evidence from your tree to build up a picture of it by making a bark rubbing with the wax crayon; drawing a simple pencil sketch; gluing in a leaf from the tree; making a pencil rubbing of a leaf.
- Back in the classroom share the findings about all the trees. Use books and the internet to identify the trees by their leaves.

Taking it further

By using some simple trigonometry the children can measure their tree and work out simple facts such as the approximate height of the tree. Begin with your back against the tree trunk, and walk away from the tree facing outwards. At regular intervals stop, bend over and look back through your legs at the tree. When you can see the top of the tree, stop. Count the large steps back to the trunk — this is the (very) approximate height of the tree in metres. Although not a very accurate measurement children love doing this.

People lines

"Children love playing this game and its variations. The less confident ones like to hold the numbers or phonemes and move about, whilst the more confident children like to boss the others about – it has something for everyone!"

By giving the children different numbers or letters to hold they can move about and become a people number line or alphabet, ordering and sorting themselves into sequences. This idea works well as a tool for Assessment for Learning too. It allows a practitioner to aim a learning objective specifically at one child or one objective at many children.

- Give the children different numerals to hold.
- Select a child to move the children to different places in the line to order the numbers in ascending order.
- Extend this further by asking the selected child to sit in a chair in front of the line and request the children holding numerals to move into position by using mathematical positional language (next to, in between, after etc.)
- By changing the numerals (11-20, even numbers, multiples of 10) then the level of challenge can be altered easily, as can the request given to the child.
- Make brief notes to record which child can achieve each type of request.

Taking it further

To make this a literacy activity, give the children phoneme cards to hold and select a child to order the phonemes alphabetically, or to spell a word by using the appropriate children. Ask a child to stand and hold either the onset or rime as a 'fixed' point. Give the remaining children some single phonemes and ask them to stand up if they could join the line to change the fixed 'at' into 'cat' – who has 'c'? Invite them to stand next to 'at' – are they on the correct side? Sound it out as a group. Repeat for other words ending in 'at'.